Reconnecting With Your Happy

MONIQUE A. CHANDLER

Published in the United States by:
Chandler Kelly Morgan Enterprises, LLC
P.O. Box 971634
El Paso, Texas 79997

ISBN: 978-0-578-17411-2

Dedications

Mom and Dad, thank you for allowing me to grow and become who I am today. My happiness and enthusiasm stems from the love and support of my family. Dad, I sincerely thank you for standing your ground and showing me the way. Mom, I sincerely thank you for always waking up in the middle of the night when I just wanted to chat. Mom and Dad, I appreciate both of you for always smiling before you pick up the phone to talk to me. I thank you so much for teaching me how to love people and respect them for who they are. I'm so delighted to have parents that are my #1 fans. I love you two more than life itself. *"Just be nice, let God fight your battles."* -Mom

My brothers, Big D, Corinthian 'Rusty', Earnell and Chris: I am forever grateful to you for believing in me and your encouragement in knowing that I could make this dream a reality. I love you guys! :-)

To all my nieces and nephews, ask God to be your anchor, remember to always say 'thank you' when someone does something nice for you, and always remember to use the southern manners your auntie taught you. I love you! :-)

To all my supportive family and friends who made it to heaven before me, you're always in my heart.

Acknowledgements

Reverend Corinthian & Rena Morgan - I am forever grateful to have you as my spiritual parents. Your unselfish love, kindness and thoughtfulness has always meant so much to me.

Mr. & Mrs. Paul Jenkins - You have been the best Godparents, and I thank you for your love.

CH/Army COL (Ret) Ronald & Shirley Strong - You set the example of what a fun loving power couple looks like. Happy we're related; I love you both. :-)

Dr. Jean DeVard-Kemp - I am grateful to you for teaching me the old school rules and how to ask for what I want.

The Messer Family from Waldo, Arkansas - Thank you for embracing me and treating me like family over the years. We have laughed at family gatherings, played games 'til the early morning hours and had a really good time. I'll never forget the love you've shown. Continue to stay connected as a family; your parents are smiling down from Heaven with joy. :-)

Joylynn M. Ross - I sincerely thank you from the bottom of my heart for editing this project. You have been there without delay and have taught me so much along the way; you are appreciated. :-)

A heartfelt loving thank you for being there for me through the years:

Harrington, Dr. Patrick, Butch, Lamar, Landon, Nate, Lorenzo, Dr. Imani, Ladorn, Susan, Hope, Corliss, Veronica F, Tami, Tammy J, Bernell, Shenay, Gloria, Tammie W-M, Veronica J-S.

What people are saying about the author and *Reconnecting With Your Happy*:

"There are few people more qualified to write a book on happiness than Monique Chandler. She is a thoughtful, intelligent, and highly motivational woman who leaves an indelible mark of joy in the hearts and minds of the people she meets. I know this book will be life changing for many people, and I am proud that Monique Chandler has decided to allow her light to shine and be shared with the world."
Dr. L. Imani Price, Ph.D.
Licensed Psychologist/Founder
Women's InnerFitness & Wellness Center
Crofton, MD
www.womeninnerfitness.com
Pink Pearls of Hope Breast Cancer Organization
Founder
www.hopeagainstbc.org

"I know Monique experienced her own life challenges over the years, but her positive attitude and determination always persevered. We can all learn to recharge and find our inner happiness at every stage of our life from Monique. Her integrity, character, and high energy level will forever set the tone and expectation for the team in our organization."
Kari Campbell, Senior VP, The Worthing Companies
www.worthingse.com

"An unknown author is credited as saying, 'People come into your life for a reason, a season, or a lifetime.' I've had my share of seasonal relationships, and along the way I've encountered people that have crossed my path for a specific reason, whether that was assisting in achieving a goal or to teach me a lesson. Monique Chandler effectively fits all categories."
Eric Ayala
Producer, Director, Author and Screenwriter.
http://www.ericayala.net/

"Monique is a natural motivator. She inspires others through her energy and enthusiasm! When you are in her presence, you feel

differently about yourself. Monique makes you realize what is impossible really spells, I'm Possible. Get connected!"
Dr. Debbie Phillips, Ph.D., CPM
Adjunct Professor Georgia Tech, Adjunct Professor UGA, Executive Director-GAIEF, President-The Quadrillion
www.thequadrillion.com

"Monique taught me the power that comes from being deliberate in choosing the type of attitude I was going to maintain throughout my life. Monique's motto of "U make it a GREAT DAY!" is simple yet powerful. Life can be difficult and complicated if you face it with a negative mindset. Monique teaches that by transforming your perspective and choosing to be happy and content, regardless of your circumstances, life can become so much more enjoyable."
Wendy M. Senior
LCSW - School Social Worker

"I am honored to have met Monique and am not surprised by this next journey of her life. Her "happy" is very real."
Dionne M. Lackey
Certified Holistic Life Coach and Founder of Wholistic Insight Now (WIN)
Co-Founder of The Wellness Xperience
www.TheWellnessXperience.com
Follow on Facebook, Twitter, Instagram and Periscope @WINwithDionne

"I have never met anyone more positive than Monique. She strives for excellence every day. Words that describe Monique are positive, driven, caring, strong, superstar, inspiring, genuine, leader, passionate, motivator, mentor, beautiful and winner! She inspires me to live life to the fullest."
Gigi Suggs
Property Manager
www.maac.com

"I found Monique's tenacity for life and service to fellow humankind unparalleled by far."
Rocky Marsh, Jr., MAED, PHR, SHRM-CP
Executive Director, Founder
High School JCAMP
www.hsjcamp.com
hsjcamp@gmail.com

"Monique is very passionate and dedicated to helping others accomplish their goals whether big or small. Her tenacity and drive is admirable. As a friend and mentor, Monique has shown me over and over how not to let the word NO be a barrier to becoming successful in my business or personal life."
Tammie Leady
Owner of Tammie Leady's Body Physiques, LLC
www.tammieleady.com
Victory1557.com

"I am impressed by Monique's ability to inspire so many people and leaving a positive impact on so many lives."
Maethea Rodgers
Property Manager

"If there is such a thing as a "Happiness Expert," Monique is certainly well qualified to don the title. Monique is well suited to help you "reconnect with your happy" because she is a living testimony of what the happy connection is all about."
Vera Jones
Speaker, Author, Broadcaster
www.verasvoiceworks.com

"In our lifetime we will meet a number of people whom we will not remember. But in that number there will only be a few people that will impact our lives in such a manner in which our life can and will change forever. Monique is one of those people. Her enthusiasm about life, her

drive in giving and supporting others motivates me and so many people who make her acquaintance. This book is sealed and filled with sincere love."
Shenay P. McCrary
Roddy Management Group, LLC

"Monique is a motivator and encourager by nature."
Iana Adrienne Patterson
Owner of All Things Possible Flowers, Occasions and More
www.atpflowershop.com

"Monique radiates positivity, and through her encouragement and life coaching, I have successfully transitioned into many opportunities. Monique Chandler's positive vision and outlook is superb and I can say without reservation, I am finally connecting with my true talent, and in the process, I am reconnecting with my Happy!"
Tamara Pray Frazier, Author/Publisher
www.thewriteonepro.com

"Monique is truly a remarkable woman destined to make everyone she works with and for GREAT."
Brandy Nasha
Wife of author, Nikki Rashan, Blogger
www.nikkiandbrandy.blogspot.com

"Monique's testimony, "Peachtree Road Race," really inspired me. People can make a difference in other's lives. I know Monique's story will make a difference."
Darrell Henderson
Toastmasters Past Area 43 Governor/ Toastmasters EPCC Club President

"With Monique's guidance and encouragement, she provides distinguished expertise on how to communicate, who to talk to, how to explain and what to accept."
James Cunningham

High School Coach

"Writing is risky. It gives voice to who you are and lets the power of your dreams emerge as an act of creation. Ask yourself, what keeps me from creating?"

Donna M. Hunter, M.A., CMHC
Weber State University
Counseling & Psychological Services Center

"Being an entrepreneur is like going to an amusement park. You go in excited and get on scary rides and fun rides. At the end of the day, you can't wait to do it all over again."

Bernell Hooker
Founder and CEO at IOU Sports and Principle Owner of Milwaukee Aces Professional Women's Basketball Team.
www.iousports.org
www.milwaukeeaces.com

Table of Content

Message from the author

I recently read a quote by Ben Sweetland that said, "Happiness is a journey, not a Destination. I think every now and then along the way we should push the PAUSE button, take a deep breath and simply enjoy being HAPPY. The day that I observed the one year anniversary of my retirement, I wanted to take a moment to celebrate my journey and the wonderful people whose teachings, advice, and kindness successfully guided me through Corporate America.

I cannot say enough about the many dedicated professionals who reached out and took me under their wings until I was ready to fly on my own, because let's face it, for every one person who is trying to build you up, there are five or six who don't want to see you succeed. I'm proud to say that I was mentored by some of the best and I will forever be in their debt because they saw something special in the seeds that my parents had planted. Instead of trying to dig them up, they cultivated and nurtured those seeds that have allowed me to grow.

Kudos to Dr. Debbie Phillips who, back in 1991, came into my life with a burst of energy and southern girl kindness. She has been one of my most influential mentors and biggest supporters for almost 25 years. When I think of her, the phrase "Each one teach one," comes to mind. Because the only thing she asks in return for all she has given is that I in turn pay it forward and teach others the many lessons she taught me.

Lamerle Howard is another integral part of my support system. Unbeknownst to me, she observed my work ethic while I was working customer service at a part-time job and asked my supervisor if she could speak with me. She told me that my parents had taught me a thing or two about kindness and she wanted me on her corporate team. I remember her telling me, "Monique, if you're coachable, I'll teach you everything you need to know to make it." I thank her for her keen eye and direct coaching style.

Pat King was a supervisor whose style was more maternal than business like. She took me and a co-worker, Maethea Rodgers, under her care and gave us the extra attention we needed as young women just starting out. She was the person who made it her mission to expose us to the little nuances and the small unspoken behaviors that we needed to reach the next level while keeping things fun and interesting.

Others who have contributed to my success and made a lasting impact on my life are Ed Buckley, Kari Campbell, Steve Jones, Tracy Bowers, Robin DeMorse, Billy "Whiteshoes" Johnson and Eric Flatterly. These guys rock, and if you all were to meet any of them, you would clearly see I am their apple and I definitely did not fall far from my corporate tree. They have been my friends, my mentors and my roots, and I thank them for holding me down as I learned to navigate my way through the business world.

Corporate America was an amazing experience, even with its many ups and downs. I can truly say I enjoyed a great run in the workforce; having fostered many lasting relationships while building an awesome resume that has allowed me to seamlessly transition into my entrepreneurial pursuits. And it gives me even more pleasure to be able to say without reservation that my corporate relationships are so solid, that should I decide to do so, I could come out of retirement at any time and find a home. I know there are some people who think I am crazy for walking away from my corporate job, but we have but one life to live, and I choose to live the life that I dream of and not the one society says I should be living. So for now, I've pushed that PAUSE button, taken a deep breath and I'm relaxing in that place called Happy!

Chapter 1
Changing Houses

The pre-teen years are times for many changes. Hormones are raging. Self-identification and self-esteem become huge factors. This is also a time when kids become less interested in family and look for approval and support from friends. Along with all of these developments of a pre-teen, the thing that I became the most proficient at was improving my argumentative skills. Not the arguing that turns into a physical altercation, but rather the arguing that would allow me to get my point across, prove that the next person was wrong and show everyone how much smarter I was than the average middle child.

No one was exempt from this immense display of brain power; not even my mother. In fact, it was one fine summer day that I had inanimately chosen to exhibit my "debating" skills against my mother. The debate was about me not wanting to follow the rules set by my parents in their home. I thought it would be great to change the rules, and desired to debate with my mother as to why the rules should be changed. Like most strong and beautiful mothers, mine commenced to putting me "in a child's place." This was followed by her telling me what I could do if I didn't like it. Boy did I not like it!

What I failed to mention earlier was that although I felt that I was always right, I couldn't escape the developmental stage of uncertainty and sensitivity that commonly accompanied a twelve year old girl. I was strong in my convictions, but sometimes weak in mind. My mother had hurt my feelings by putting me in a child's place, and I wasn't happy.

"I'm leaving," I announced. Scary thoughts ran through my mind about being out there on the streets alone, but I was determined that I would win the battle.

My declaration didn't garner the response that I had expected from my mother. In fact, there was no reaction at all. She simply walked away as if the conversation had never happened. I ran into the kitchen to find the biggest brown paper sack to pack my things in. Bag in hand, I stomped my way to my bedroom. I needed a plan. I would go far away and live with someone who knew how smart I was and would not say things that hurt my feelings. One by one, I began opening and closing the drawers that held my t-shirts, shorts and underwear. I made sure to make as much noise as possible. I wanted my mother to know that I was serious.

Several minutes later, my mother appeared in the doorway of my self-decorated bedroom. My bedroom was painted bright pink and the walls were neatly covered with cutout pages framed from *Ebony*, *Right On!* and *Vogue* magazines.

"You need some help?" Mom asked with a sincere, loving voice. My mother was always patient with me regardless of what I was going through in my own little world.

Help? Did she just offer to help me pack? Did she want me to leave? I didn't answer my mother. I continued to fold each item and neatly stuff them into my bag. My mother sat at the foot of my bed and began to assist me in packing my things.

"Don't forget your toothbrush," she stated.

My eyes began to well up with tears, but I refused to cry. I don't think I blinked for a minute straight, because I knew once my lids joined, the tears would be pushed out and I'd look like a pre-teen. This was not the time for me to look like a pre-teen; not when I was trying to be a teenager.

My mother continued to help me pack without saying a word.

All kinds of crazy thoughts swirled around my adolescent brain as I progressed in preparing to leave home. Did she want me to leave? Was she really going to allow me to walk out that door? Did *I* really want to walk out that door?

After leaving my eyes open for so long in order to dry up the tears, they eventually subsided to the point where I could blink them away before they had a chance to slide down my cheeks. After that, I completed the task at hand. I was determined to prove to my mother that she had not won.

"Done," I said after I put the final piece of clothing into the bag. I looked at my mother with wanting eyes. I wanted her to grab my clothes filled paper sack. I wanted her to ask me not to leave. I wanted her to put her arms around me and say, "You are so smart," or "I'm sorry."

Needless to say, that's not what she said or did. Patting me on the leg, my mother arose from my bed and left the room. I stood there several minutes before taking a step, feeling like my best friend had just moved away.

The walk from my bedroom to the front door had never been so long. I slowly moved through my house hoping that with the next step, I would hear my mother's voice telling me to stop playing around and go to my room. I took long glances at every wall, every piece of furniture, and all of our family portraits. One of my favorite portraits was of my parents, my siblings and me, along with our grandparents and Cousin Jesse and her poodle, who had been visiting from New Jersey. I was going to miss my house, my room, my siblings and my parents. My entire life was going to change because I was changing houses.

Before reaching the front door, I heard my mother's voice. She had finally come to her senses and was going to beg me to stay.

"Where are you going?" she calmly asked.

"Far away from here," I exclaimed, and I knew just how I was going to get there.

I had the best red princess bike in the world. It was beautiful. It had a white basket with colorful flowers on the front of the handlebars. It was perfect for carrying my belongings. I really thought that bicycle would take me to the moon if I ever wanted to go.

My mother pressed past me and politely opened the front door. I was leaving home and she didn't seem to be worried at all. I hopped on my bike and headed to my destination. There was no stopping me now . . . Not that I hadn't wished someone would stop me.

Two blocks and five minutes later, I arrived at my destination. My grandparents didn't seem surprised to see me. With my brown paper sack in my arms, I told them that I'd had it with my mother and had run away from home. They took me in with no questions asked. I made myself comfortable in my very own guestroom before approaching my visiting cousins. I explained that none of the kids were to tell my dad that I'd run away from home when he showed up at my grandparents'.

Like clockwork, my dad stopped by my grandparents'—his parents'—house on his way home from work. His truck pulled into the driveway and I took cover in my "new room." I soon found out that my cousin Andrew couldn't keep a secret for any amount of candy in the world. However, my dad made me feel like I was really gone, and therefore was no longer of his concern. He visited with my grandparents as if nothing had changed. Rich voices of community going-ons and talk of sports filled the air.

Two hours had passed and I began to wonder if my dad wanted me gone from the home, too, just as my mother had. I heard him saying his good-byes. As my father was leaving, he knocked on the guestroom door. I didn't answer.

"Monique," he said through the closed door. "I know you're here. You just take a few days and we'll see you back at home."

I smiled because I was a daddy's girl and he loved me without judging my actions. Daddy didn't spank me or raise his voice at me. He called me his chocolate drop princess.

I stayed at my grandparents' house all of two nights before riding my bike back home. I had gotten homesick by then. I missed my room, my siblings, my dad and my house. Most of all, I missed my mother. While at my grandparents' house, there was no cable television or fun games to play. My cousins eventually went home, so there were no kids to play with or talk to (although I wasn't talking to Andrew). Going anyplace fun was not going to happen. My grandparents loved being at home.

As I returned home with a new brown paper sack filled with dirty clothes, my mother greeted me at the front door.

"Guess who decided to return home?" she sarcastically announced. She took my bag from me and led me into the family room where my dad was waiting. My parents had a long talk with me about my behavior and actions.

During this two hour lecture, my parents questioned me about what I was thinking and what I had accomplished by running away. They counseled me on what I should do the next time I was upset or embarrassed.

They told me that I would have to learn to deal with my problems in a more effective manner.

When I asked my mother why she didn't stop me from running away, she simply replied, "I legally have no way to make you stay." Now that I'm older and understand that whippings are frowned upon by some members of society, I know that in all actuality what my mother was saying was that she wasn't going to chance going to jail for beating me down. LOL!

You see, my mother refused to give my behavior power. My parents told me that they loved me very much and they expected me to make better decisions. "Take responsibility now or you'll be running for the rest of your life," my father said.

As a consequence to my actions, my parents had me write a three page paper about responsibility and accountability. As I finished reading aloud my handwritten letter to my parents, my mother sighed in relief. She rose to her feet and put her soft arms around my body in a strong embrace. My mother looked at me with her gentle eyes and said, "Life is what you make it, Monique."

I never forgot those words. I reminded myself of those words when girls in high school were running around with older guys and found themselves pregnant months later. No, it didn't stop those girls from succeeding in life, but it did add additional responsibilities that didn't need to take place so early on in their lives. I also watched girls getting pregnant in college and having to drop out to take care of their child. As college students, we were offered free Planned Parenthood care, and very few of us took advantage of the free preventative care service.

Sometimes always trying to be right and doing what you want to do . . . Well . . . Has its consequences. But we are all equipped to make choices for a better life, even as pre-teens, so by the time we are grown, we should have this thing mastered!

Chapter 2
Making Candles

I always thought of myself as a very creative person. Whether it was making ordinary things look beautiful, or taking a fancy thing and making it fabulous, I had the magic touch. However, on one particular summer day, my creative mojo made a big stink . . . Literally!

"Want to go for a ride, baby girl?"

My dad knew how much I loved going with him for rides in his truck since all of the women in our family drove cars. I didn't hesitate to hop inside his truck and ride into town with him.

On our way back from town, my dad decided to stop by the home of one of his construction buddies. This particular friend and his wife had a ton of kids. The youngest daughter was 12 years old, just a few years older than me. There was hardly an introduction before she and I raced down the hall and into the kids' playroom. It was very rare that I made friends outside of my large family. However, Retania and I hit it off very well. I knew then that we would be great friends.

"Do you want to color?" Retania asked me, holding a box of crayons in her hand.

"Sure, but what are we going to color?" I looked around the room. "Where are your coloring books?" I replied.

She began searching the toy box, the closet and other places around the playroom. She looked high and low. "I can't find my coloring books!" Retania exclaimed.

At that moment, as I stared at the crayons she held, there must have been a half-lit lightbulb that went off inside of my head. "Let's make candles!" I declared my bright idea. "We can make them out of crayons. I can show you how."

Retania agreed to my suggestion and we quickly gathered all of the crayons that we could find.

Next I told her we needed to go to the kitchen. As we walked into the kitchen, I noticed that my father and her parents were hanging out on the front porch.

Retania suggested that we let the grown-ups know what we were about to do, or at least go outside to get her older brothers and sisters to help. I convinced her that because I didn't know how much longer my father would be visiting, that there was no time to waste. Then I assured her that I knew exactly what I was doing and that she needn't worry. I had actually learned the task of making candles from watching a television show after school one afternoon. It was my pleasure to pass on the knowledge.

We sat at the kitchen table and broke up all the crayons. After we placed the broken crayons in a cooking pot, Retania turned on the front burner of the stove. The crayons began to melt over the heat and we were soon on our way to creating beautiful candles, or so we thought.

Shortly after our "candles" began to cook, something strange happened. A very strong, unpleasant odor emerged from the pot. That odor traveled throughout the house and to the outside, alarming the adults.

Retania became afraid. I assured her that everything was okay.

"It's supposed to smell like that," I said. "It's okay," I reassured her, but it wasn't. As a matter of fact, it was anything but okay. But I'd mastered, even at this young of age, keeping others cool and calm during an otherwise catastrophic time.

Retania's father came running into the kitchen. "What is that smell?" he screamed. He looked to his daughter. "Retania, what is going on?"

Retania stood frozen while I proudly announced, "We're making candles. They just didn't come out quite right."

My father apologized to his buddy and ordered me out the door. With a slight smile and a wave goodbye to my new friend, I headed out the front door.

That particular ride home with my father seemed to be the longest ride ever. He proceeded to lecture me about safety and fire hazards. My father put me on restriction from our own kitchen, as I was only allowed to enter after clearing the dishes from our dining room table.

When my mother got wind of what I had done, she handed me the house phone and demanded that I call to apologize to Retania and her parents. Retania's parents accepted my apology.

When I got off the phone my mother then asked, "I hope you learned a lesson, young lady."

"I did," I assured her. "Next time I will just use old candle wax instead." Needless to say, after I made that comment and my mother rebutted it, there was no next time.

Chapter 3
Family, Love & Togetherness

"Thank you! Thank you! Thank you!" I said to my audience as I blew kisses to the crowd and proceeded to bow. "Oh you all are too kind." I wrapped my feather boa around my neck dramatically as I exited the stage. I was overwhelmed with excitement as I concluded my concert. "Did you all enjoy the show?" I asked the audience as I reentered the stage area looking from one face to the next. "Let's give it up for Monique as Ms. Natalie Cole!" I imagined the massive applause coming from the crowd.

"Monique!" Mom called. "Child, what are you doing in here with all of these dolls and stuffed animals all over the place?" she asked before picking up two of my dolls. She looked around my bedroom. Her eyebrows raised when saw the mud pies I'd made to feed my guests.

"Mommy, I was doing a show," I protested. "I am doing a Natalie Cole concert today."

Mom giggled. "Last week it was Diana Ross, now this week it's Natalie. My little song bird," she replied. "I hate to break up your show, Miss Cole, but it's time to clean up for dinner. You've gotta put all these dolls away and take these mud pies back on the front porch before your daddy gets home," she said before walking into the kitchen.

I slowly began to pick up my dolls and put them away. As I cleaned up, I hummed a happy tune. I loved music, and as The O'Jays would say, *any kind of music*!

"Mo, why don't you sing us all a song," Daddy said one evening after everyone had finished eating dinner.

I saw my sister, Lisa, roll her eyes and my little brother giggled.

"Okay, Daddy," I replied. "What do you want to hear?" I was thrilled at the prospect of putting on a show for a live audience.

"How about a little bit of Diana Ross and the Supremes?" he said before taking a sip of his southern sweet iced tea.

"Daddy, do we have to listen to her sing?" my brother whined.

"Yea, Cousin Khak, do we have to?" my cousin, Butch, who was joining us for dinner, seconded.

"Yes, you have to listen," Daddy said. "My chocolate drop is going to be the next Natalie Cole." He looked to me. "Right, Sweetie?"

"Yep, I am gonna be famous just like her! I'm gonna wear fur coats, too, and everyone is gonna come to my concerts," I said before I ran to my room to get my microphone.

"That child loves to sing more than anyone I know," I heard Mom tell my dad as I was coming back into the room. And she was right. I couldn't carry a tune in a bucket, but I didn't care. I loved music, and if there was ever an opportunity to sing to a live audience, I was ready. And since my daddy wanted me to sing, then I was gonna sing. They all better plug their ears because I was about to put on the show of the century.

"Stop! In the name of love and my eardrums," my sister yelled while putting her hands over her ears.

"Momma, make her stop," my brother said as I began singing yet another Supremes' melody.

"Cut it out, she's doing a good job." Mom admonished my siblings and cousin with a stern look.

"Baby, baby, where did our love go?" I sang.

Daddy and Mom watched me proudly while Lisa, Big D and Cousin Butch tried to hide their displeasure.

"Sing, Baby Girl," Daddy prodded me on as I worked the room, refusing to disappoint.

For as long as I can remember, I've loved music. Every time either of my parents had errands to run, I would be the first person to jump into our Ford Torino and turn on the radio. I would sing whatever songs came on the radio like I was the original artist. I knew all the words to almost every song that played, but I especially liked Diana Ross and Natalie Cole. They were both so beautiful and glamorous. I couldn't wait to grow up so I could be just like them. While my singing left a lot to be desired, I still felt like I could be famous, and I'm certain I got on my parents' nerves with my constant howling. But they never complained; at least not to my face.

Both of my parents were big music fans, and whenever a concert would come to Jacksonville, they would make sure to be front and center. I envied the fact that they were able to see all of their favorite singers. I used to beg Daddy to take me with them, but he would just whisper in my ear, "I can't take you tonight, but tomorrow on Saturday, I will take the whole family to the drive-in movie, and we can go get ice cream after church from Tasty Freeze on Sunday."

Daddy knew as much as I loved music, I couldn't resist Tasty Freeze, and that would usually satisfy me. In hindsight I now realize their concert dates was their time alone without us kids.

"Guess what, Mo?" Mom asked as she walked into my room with Cousin Butch.

"Ma'am?" I asked in return as she knelt down beside my bed.

"Guess who is going to the James Brown concert?" she asked me with excitement.

"You and Daddy are going to see James Brown!" I shrieked. "Ooh, Mommy, I like when he sings "Papa's Got a Brand New Bag," I said as I jumped up and slid across the floor and attempted to do a James Brown split.

Cousin Butch and Mom both laughed at me when I got stuck on the floor and couldn't get back up.

"Girl, you are something else," Cousin Butch said. "A little singing, dancing machine." He laughed.

Mom came over and helped me up from the floor and said, "Not Daddy and me, but Monique and me!"

I squealed so loud that my mom dropped me back on the floor to cover her ears.

We showed up at the concert early so we could get a good spot on the floor close to the stage. Yes, the tickets were assigned seats, but the early folks would go down on the floor to take close-up pictures of the entertainers before taking their seats. I was so excited to be there. Mom had made me a pair of red polyester pants and a black shirt, and for the occasion, I got to wear my black one inch heels. I thought I was the stuff! I had my hair in two afro puffs and you couldn't tell me nothing!

When James Brown took the stage, I got extra excited, and not just because of his singing. James Brown had on the same exact outfit as me, and as excited as I was to discover this, he was equally excited. He looked out and saw me standing there with stars in my eyes and he immediately pointed to me and said, "Mr. Rocc, bring her up here." Mr. Rocc was a 6'9" bodyguard. He escorted me onto the stage to showcase my outfit. I was thrilled to both be on stage, and to meet James Brown. I felt like Mr. Rocc was my own personal bodyguard.

I was so happy to be standing on stage with the Godfather of Soul. I felt like I must've been the luckiest 10 year old alive.

Before I turned 18, I had been to more concerts than most people will attend in a lifetime. Because of my habit of getting there early and getting a spot near the stage, I had the opportunity to touch hands with Rick James, Teena Marie, Tina Turner, and Prince! I was excited when I got a friendly wink from Teddy Pendergrass and Marvin Gaye, but Randy Jackson really, really winked at me . . . You know, wink-wink like a boy winks at a girl he likes. Now that kind of wink made my teenage heart swoon! You couldn't tell me I wasn't going to marry at least one member of the Jackson 5! Shoot, Randy winked at ME . . . not anyone else, just me, Monique, the concert queen!

Every time the doors of the Jacksonville Coliseum opened, I was standing in line with either my sister, my older cousins or my parents. I was determined not to miss a concert.

Over the years, I have expanded my taste in music. I've been exposed to different genres and I enjoy listening to a little bit of everything. YES, I still love to sing, and, NO, I haven't gotten any better at it. I'm still the concert queen, but now I travel all over the country in search of a good concert. I've been to the Rock n' Roll Festival in Virginia, as well as a Country Music Festival in Nashville. I've seen the Doobie Brothers, Sonny

& Cher, Donnie & Marie and Michael McDonald. It has been my pleasure to attend the Kool Jazz Festival in Atlanta where I was able to see Patti Labelle, the Commodores and my childhood favorite, Diana Ross. I've lived a life full of music and joy!

One of my fondest memories was at a family reunion held at my Aunt Ellen's house. She lived Cross the Creek in Florida and I absolutely loved when our family would get together and sing and dance in the yard. I remember performing some of my high school dance routines to one of my favorite songs, "Love Will Keep Us Together," by Captain & Tennille. They were one of my favorite duos.

I remember that day in Aunt Ellen's yard; I sang the daylights out of that song as I kicked up my legs and shimmied through my dance routine, oblivious to the fact that everyone was frowning at my suspect singing voice. But as I already stated, I didn't care because I just loved to sing. Singing was always a good time for me, but believe it or not, my favorite pastime almost got me in a bunch of trouble one time.

Mom, Grandma Tiny, my brother and I were traveling to Jacksonville one afternoon. Big D and I were in the backseat pretending to be Captain & Tennille, singing "Love Will Keep Us Together." We were

34

having the best time putting on a concert for the trucker who was traveling behind us. My mom put on her left blinker to turn into the mall, and I turned around and signaled to the trucker that he should turn in behind us. Low and behold, he did just that!

When we parked, the trucker pulled up behind us and got out of the truck. I don't know what his intentions were, but after my Grandma Tiny got through giving him a "word of encouragement," he was more than happy to get back in his truck and "take a ride," as my grandmother had put it that day. My brother and I were so shocked; we never did anything like that again!

As lyricist B.J. Thomas said in his song "I Believe in Music," "Music is the universal language and love is the key to brotherhood, peace and understanding; livin' in harmony," and I truly believe that. Some of the best times of my life have been spent with family and friends (who are like family), sitting around singing songs and sharing laughter. And as long as we were making music, there didn't seem to be a care in the world . . . Just good old fashioned Family, Love & Extraordinary Togetherness!

Chapter 4
Running From a Spanking

Throughout most of my school aged life, my cousins and I would spend our summers playing at my grandparents' house. They resided in a small country town in Florida. Although my grandparents didn't live on a farm, they owned pigs, hogs, and chickens. My grandparents had seventeen children. My dad and eleven of his brothers, lovingly referred to as "The Boys," would chip in on grocery money and go to their parents' home daily for a hot lunch prepared with love by the aunts. No one cared how much food anybody ate, because there was always plenty. We were all very close and learned from each of our parents to take care of one another.

There were so many cousins that we really didn't have anyone outside of the family come over to play. The two youngest uncles, Michael and Greg, would hang out and play with us during the summer. They both were close in age to some of the older cousins.

One summer morning I awoke with my cousins at my grandparents' home. We had cereal and oatmeal before heading out back to work on our playhouse we had started building the day before. This particular house was being built with old household furniture and some abandoned pots and pans that we had found around the neighborhood.

Time had flown by so fast that we were all surprised to hear my grandmother call us in for lunch. We ran inside to wash our hands and prepare to eat. As we all lined up to receive our peanut butter and jelly sandwich and cup of Kool-Aid, I noticed something out of the ordinary. Uncle Greg was not at the front of the line behind Uncle Michael like he usually was. Just as I started to wonder where he was, Uncle Greg appeared. He was sweaty and out of breath, but had a slightly mischievous smile on his face. All of the cousins began to question Uncle Greg regarding his appearance and his whereabouts.

"Where have you been?" I whispered.

"I was playing with the chickens," he replied, then winked.

As the last of the kids sat down in the grass under the pecan trees, while some sat under the pine trees with their sandwiches and drinks, The Boys began pulling up in their trucks. Hot lunches were awaiting them inside for their hour-long lunch break from work.

Granny had been out in the backyard hanging wet, clean clothes on the handmade clotheslines to dry. The telephone rang and Granny disappeared into the house to answer it. Shortly thereafter, she reappeared back outside with a frown on her face and her eyebrows furrowed.

Granny inquired, "Which one of you kids let out the chickens?"

No one answered.

Uncle Ross took over the interrogation. "Who let the chickens out?" he yelled.

We all continued eating our sandwiches and gulping down our drinks. We knew that Uncle Greg was responsible, but we wouldn't dare tell on one another. That was an unspoken family rule amongst us youngsters.

"Okay, if no one is going to speak up, then all of you will get a spanking," Uncle Ross declared.

Was Uncle Ross serious? Was he really going to spank *all* of us?

As I continued to question my uncle's rationale, he motioned for my cousins and me to stand in a single file line to get a spanking. I had to do something!

Think, Monique, think!

I loved my cousins and we had a bond, but I was not about to get a spanking with them for something that I hadn't done. Clearly I was the only one who felt this way, as one by one, my cousins stepped up to Uncle Ross and received a spanking. Afterward, each one of them walked away in tears.

I was third to the back of the line and getting closer. Time was running out, so that's when I decided that I was going to take off running before it was my turn for a spanking. I knew from our family gatherings that Uncle Ross was quick and quite the athlete, so I had to act fast. My cousin Freda was seven cousins ahead of me. That would give me just the jumpstart I needed on Uncle Ross if he tried to catch me.

Just as Uncle Ross was in mid-swing with one of the other cousins, I made a mad dash. I ran past the other cousins, around the lunch garbage bags, through the yard, down the driveway, across the street, around the corner and into my house. My house and my grandparents' house were in walking distance of each other, but I *ran*! I ran all the way home as fast as my feet would move. I didn't return to my grandparents' house for an entire week; until I was sure things had died down and Uncle Ross had forgotten that he owed me a spanking.

There were several lessons learned for me in this incident. Having closeness like brothers and sisters and being loyal as a whole regardless of any circumstance was amazingly beautiful. The cousins' loyalty ran very strong. I struggled, just as many young people, with understanding when to be loyal versus doing what's right. Because the cousins and I were asked the question about who had let the chickens out as a group, I didn't feel the need to step up and answer. If we had been asked individually, I probably would have told the truth. Why? Because there would have been no one else around to ridicule or say anything about my choice. Even as adults, no matter how much we say, "I don't care what people think of me," we really do . . . As we should. Running from the situation may not have been the best choice in this matter, but it saved me from a spanking!

When I finally returned to my grandparents', neither my uncle Ross nor any of the adult family members mentioned anything else about the chickens. My cousins, Renee and Wanda, teased me for a few days because I was the only nonathletic cousin known to man, but that day I had run like I was training for the Summer Olympics. My mother's saying in our household was, "You can do what's right and enjoy a fruitful life, or you can do what you want and face the consequences." Needless to say, it's now one of the sayings I live by.

Chapter 5
Lessons Learned

Life has taught me many lessons. The avenues for learning these lessons have come in many forms. Many of those avenues for me were certain people. Of those people, there were educators, family, friends, and most importantly, my parents. One very important lesson that my parents taught me was the value of a dollar.

My parents began teaching my siblings and me this lesson at a young age. Initially I never really understood why we had to deal with money issues as children. I can remember the very first time that I received an allowance. It was a Thursday evening after my father had come home from work. We all sat in the family room and my parents handed each of us ten one dollar bills. The following Friday before leaving for the rival football game, we were summoned into the dining room. My father was sitting at one head of the table and my mother at the other. My siblings and I sat around them with bewildered looks on our faces. My parents explained that we would each have to give our mother three dollars for food. Additionally, we would have to give our father three dollars for room and board.

"Why?" I asked.

My father quickly responded, "You always have to have a place to stay. And you always have to have food on the table."

But why do we have to pay back our allowance? I thought. However, the sternness in my father's response let me know that I didn't need to question his logic. I reluctantly gave up the six dollars. I was even more disturbed when my father reminded us all that we would have to put a dollar of our allowance in the church tithes and offering basket on Sunday. I used my fingers and counted down from ten. I would only have three dollars to spare. I just didn't get it. We were the children!

Every week our family repeated this routine, and every week I reluctantly gave up six dollars of my allowance to my parents. I quickly began to think of ways that I could have more money by the week's end. As a kid, I looked forward to every weekend. We would always go somewhere as a family. I often voted to go to the mall. Sometimes I would get my way and other times not. After a while, it didn't matter where we went, because we would have just as much fun at the zoo, the park or a ball game.

On Saturdays my brother would wake up craving *Now or Later* candy. Surprisingly, my father would allow my brother to buy his favorite candy at 10:45 a.m. My father would say, "Son, you can buy that candy out of your allowance."

After saving my own three dollars, I asked my brother, "Why don't you wait until noon when dad buys us dessert with our lunch?" I explained to him that he would be able to keep his three dollars by choosing the *Now or Later* candy as his dessert. Of course my brother didn't understand. He wanted his candy *now* and not later. At noon I would get my cherry flavored Slush Puppy, compliments of my dad, and keep three dollars in my pocket. This money managing routine went on throughout my teenage years.

On high school graduation night, my parents presented me with gifts. My father first handed me a small box that was neatly wrapped. I sat on the edge of the couch and slowly unraveled the ribbons. Upon opening the box, I reached inside to pull out a small wooden ladder, along with a card. I wasn't sure what I was supposed to do with this small wooden ladder, so I opened the card. In my father's small, neat print it read, *"Don't ever forget the same people that you passed going up the ladder, will be the same people you will pass coming down."* Inside that card was a check made out to me in the amount of $9,000. I was elated. Just as I began to wonder why my father had written me a check for so much money, I looked into the left-hand corner where it had the word "memo." Next to that my father had written, *"For Room & Board."* I hugged my father's neck.

My mother then handed me a box that was slightly bigger. I took the same care to open this box. As I opened the box I noticed that inside was a wooden horse. Now I was confused. I understood the concept of the ladder, but didn't quite understand the toy horse. But sure enough there was a card to go along with this gift. The card read, *"Don't ever forget how to come down off that high horse!"* My mother knew me all too well. Much to my surprise, there was a check inside of the card from my mother. The check was also made out to me in the amount of $9,000. The bottom left hand corner of this check read, *"For Food."* I couldn't believe my parents had saved all the money I had "contributed to the household" over the years.

After walking across the stage to receive my diploma, I looked into the crowd at my parents. I thought about the wisdom that they had and how they used that wisdom to teach my siblings and me valuable lessons about life. By giving us an allowance, my parents taught us how to manage money. They also taught us how to save money. Through application we learned how to spend money and what to buy and what not to buy (and when to buy it). To this day, I can truly say that I know how to manage money because of the lessons learned from my loving parents.

Chapter 6
All Hogs Go to Heaven

On a beautiful spring morning when I was in middle school, I got up early and decided to visit my Grandma Chandler's house so I could hang out and play with my cousins. I was on spring break and had made plans for the entire weekend. I was so excited to start my holiday.

Later on that night I was going to the local fair with my older cousins, and then the following day I was headed to Walt Disneyworld in Orlando. From there I was going to visit Busch Gardens in Tampa. I was looking forward to visiting the parks, but for the moment, the only thing I could think about was getting to Grandma's house so I could enjoy some of her delicious breakfast.

I stood in the mirror staring at my reflection. I turned to the left and then turned to the right to admire my outfit. I had gotten my hair braided the night before and I really liked the way it was styled. I smiled at my pink fingernails that my cousin, Freda, had polished. They were the perfect match for the cute pink dress and sandals my mom helped me put together. I was looking so darn cute that I couldn't wait to show off my outfit.

When I got to Grandma Chandler's house, Miss Cynt, my daddy's cousin, served all of us kids a huge breakfast outside at the picnic table under the pecan and oak trees. Everything was so delicious, and even though we were full, we decided to play chase to see who was the fastest. I was not dressed for this type of play, but I was always ready for a game of chase— sandals or no sandals. We used the garden as our track and began racing up and down the field between the rows of corn on the cob, bell peppers, sugarcane and peas. As I stood between the rows of corn and sugarcane, I called out, "On your mark, get set, ready . . . Go!" and I took off like the wind! We were having so much fun running and laughing, that we barely heard when we were called.

"Kids!" a loud voice continued to call out from the back porch. Miss Cynt stood at the back door until she saw us running toward the porch. The swill was there for us to feed the hogs. All of my aunts and uncles would bring over their leftovers to add to the buckets to make swill, and when it was ready, Grandma counted on us kids to make sure the hogs were fed. We grabbed the swill—two kids per bucket—and slowly carried it out to the hog pen.

"Monique, I don't know why you have on that dress," my cousin Valeria mumbled as we were struggling to tote the bucket. "You gotta keep stopping every five seconds," she complained, as I, for the umpteenth time, gently put down my side of the bucket.

I looked at her but decided to ignore her comment. I was not going to spill any of that nasty slop on my dress no matter how long it took for us to get there.

"Come on," I said while grabbing my side of the bucket. "Let's get finished so I can get back to beating you down the field." I laughed.

All of my male cousins dumped the swill in the trough and the girls stood watching as the hogs began sloshing through the mud and vying for a spot around the trough. For some reason I decided to climb the fence and sit on the top wire to watch the hogs. I wanted a front row, up close and personal view I suppose. Never mind I had on my cute, pink dress and sandals. I wanted to sit on the fence, so I did. All of my cousins were yelling at me to get down. I heard Valerie and Wanda say, "Monique, you better get off that fence before you fall in that hog pen!"

I looked down at them with a huge smile on my face. I was on top of the world when all of a sudden I lost my balance. Yep, I tumbled down right into the mud!

"Aaaah!" I screamed as I hit the ground with a loud thud.

Within seconds I was surrounded by a few of the hogs. I was lying face down in the mud in total shock and embarrassment, thinking I was about to be trampled by a bunch of hogs. I was attempting to get up when I heard laughter and snickering as a few of my cousins made an effort to open the gate to help me.

"Help!" I cried as I slipped back down in the mud again. I looked up and saw *Man* making his way over to me. Man was the biggest hog in the pen; tipping the scales at about 489 pounds. He had always been my favorite "pet," but at that moment, I didn't want us to be in such close proximity.

I closed my eyes, imagining the worst when I felt a wet feeling on the side of my face. I peeked out and noticed it was Man and a few other hogs licking my face and hair. As my cousins rushed in, the hogs continued to try to lick all the mud off of me. That set my cousins off with another round of laughter.

"Ewww, look at them licking her," one of my cousins said and then pointed, as my other cousins, Lafayette and Ricky, helped me out of the pen.

"Oh my goodness! What in the world happened to you?" Miss Cynt shouted as I stood in the backdoor covered from head to toe in stinky mud.

"She fell in the hog pen," my cousin Jacquelyn explained; as if an explanation was needed.

I could see in Miss Cynt's eyes that she wanted to laugh, but she held it in as she walked to the rear of the house and came back with some old towels. "Go out to the spigot, Monique," she said. "I better get you cleaned up before your mama sees you, and we sure can't do it inside," she said as she walked outside behind me.

I had a change of clothes over at Grandma's house, so after I got cleaned up, Cousin Wanda took my hair loose, shampooed it, and then braided it again. I felt so much better, but boy was I filled with regret and embarrassment. Of course I was the butt of jokes for a few days, but the only thing hurting was my pride.

However, I steered clear of the hog pen for a while and didn't go out there until about a month later. I decided that I needed to talk to the hogs and tell them thank you for taking care of me, so I made my way to the fence. I stood there calling out Man's name. I wanted to thank him especially for initiating trying to clean me up.

"Man," I yelled out a few more times, but he never came to the fence.

I looked around a little bit longer and then a terrible thought hit me. I took off running into the house and looked into the freezer. Low and behold, Man's head was staring back at me.

"Grandma!" I yelled as I stared at the huge hog head in the freezer. Ricky came up behind me and I turned to him and said, "How could they kill Man? He was our pet!"

Ricky looked at me and said in a matter of fact tone, "No, he wasn't a pet. He was meat and we're gonna make some hog head cheese *and* it's gonna be reaaallll good too."

I ran out the house heartbroken because I had always looked at the farm animals as pets, not food for slaughter. It upset me terribly that this was going to happen again and again. I decided to stop eating meat, as if that would stop them from dying. I managed to go without eating meat for a long time . . . Until the lure of the bacon became too much and I fell off the wagon.

I had to come to the realization that the purpose for raising animals was for them to provide sustenance for us, but I never forgot my hog pen experience and the day my pet hog, Man, took such good care of me. After his death I was filled with so much heartbreak and regret. Because of my silly, childish pride, I let a whole month go by before I went back to tell him thank you for taking care of me . . . And by then, it was too late.

This is something that I see happening all the time. We always think we have tomorrow. "Oh, I will call her tomorrow," or "I will tell her I'm sorry tomorrow." We wait to tell our loved ones "I'm sorry," "thank you," or "I love you," and in some instances, it's too late because we never know what heartbreak tomorrow may bring.

We should never ever allow pride, time, distance or any other reason stop us from acknowledging our loved ones and those who are there for us in our lives. Give them their flowers while they can still enjoy them.

As for my favorite pet, Man, well . . . I think about him often and it's been my constant prayer and belief that All Pet Hogs Go to Heaven!

Chapter 7
When You Do Wrong, You Pay the Price

Early one hot summer morning, I was awakened by my father. I was lying soundly asleep in bed when he came into my room and whispered, "Monique? Your mom and I are heading off to work."

I rolled over and gave my father a sleepy smile.

"Grandma Tiny will be looking in on you guys this week," he said. "I want you all to be on your best behavior." He turned to leave my room, but before doing so he added, "Oh, and by the way, Cousin Charles just waxed the floors down at RJE Gym." Robinson Jenkins Ellis School was known by folks as RJE. The history of the school is that it was the only one for Blacks in the area back in the day. To this day the gym is still being used to play city league basketball, and the baseball field is used as well. "You guys stay away from there today."

"Yes, Daddy," I replied.

My mother was the first to leave. Shortly thereafter I heard the door to my father's truck close and him driving off. I hadn't laid in that bed another minute before a thought jumped into my head, causing me to pop right out of bed and burst into my brother's room.

"Dad said that Cousin Charles just waxed the gym floor and that we shouldn't go down there today," I relayed to my brother excitedly. One would have thought I would have been a little bit disappointed to say the least, but not with the thoughts I had brewing. My brother didn't share my excitement. He didn't respond because, low and behold, he was still asleep.

I decided to shake him. "Wake up! Did you hear what I said?" I could hardly contain myself. "The gym floor is freshly waxed! We should go down there and skate!" I figured the floor would be easier to skate on leveled with a top coat of wax. We were going to have some summer fun.

"If the floor is waxed, then the gym is closed," my brother said in a groggy and irritated voice. "Leave me alone." He pulled his blanket over his head.

I couldn't stop thinking about how much fun it would be to get on that gym floor in my skates. No, we had not skated inside RJE's gym before. The gym was always off limits to kids unless there was a game or activity taking place. But I thought it would be a great first time, because we could possibly fly off the wax and do some fun skating drills.

After lunch with Grandma Tiny, I made my way outdoors with skates in hand. It didn't take much to convince my brother to tag along. I never went skating without him. We saw a few cousins and kids in the neighborhood along the way.

"Hey guys, RJE Gym is open today. We should go down there and skate!" I exclaimed.

Soon after, my brother and I, along with a group of cousins and neighborhood kids, were headed to the gym to skate. When we arrived, the floor was nice and shiny and better than any skating rink we had ever attended. We glided across the shiny new wonderland. We raced forward and backward, to and from. We were having a great time. No sooner than we were well into our skating excursion, there was a loud yell.

"Hey, what are you kids doing on that floor?!"

We all looked to see a member of the management team, good ole Cousin Charles, standing in the doorway to the gym.

Immediately the gym filled with all kinds of ruckus and confusion. All the kids were frightened by Cousin Charles and they were crying out loud and skating really fast to get out of the gym before he recognized them and told their parents. One kid was even pleading with Cousin Charles not to call his parents because he'd be grounded for the rest of the summer. As the volume in the gym began to rise, so did I, my feet anyway. They flew up toward the ceiling after coming from underneath my body.

My arms made direct contact with the floor as I tried to use them to break my fall. My arms were throbbing and I wasn't able to move. I was so stunned and in so much pain.

Cousin Charles and a friend of one of my uncle's on my dad's side of the family came to my rescue. Tears began to stream from my eyes. I had never been in this much pain in my life. All the other kids were told to go home and not to come back to the gym until their parents were notified.

Cousin Charles was working and couldn't leave the gym unattended. The family friend that happened to be at the gym offered to take me to my dad's job.

"No!" I screamed between sobs. "Please no. Take me to my mom's job!" I would rather go to my mom's job because I knew there was a chance that she might be more nurturing and compassionate. My dad would be compassionate only *after* he explained how disappointed he was in me. I did not like to nor did I ever want to disappoint my dad. I was a bonafide "Daddy's Girl."

Cousin Charles and my uncle helped me up as our family friend led me to his car. On the ride over to my mother's job, I couldn't stop thinking about how much trouble I had gotten myself into.

"You kids are crazy to skate on that waxed floor. Do you know how bad you could have hurt yourself?" the family friend scolded. "You're eleven years old now. You should know better."

I was getting a ride and a lecture. However, I knew that the fussing out I had coming from my parents would be far worse.

We pulled up to my mother's job. "You stay here and I'll go inside and get your mom," I was told.

My heart skipped a beat. I could only imagine how my mother was going to react to some strange man coming to her job to tell her that her daughter was hurt. My dad and all of his brothers knew my uncle's friend, but my mother had never met him.

Soon my mother came running to the car. "What did your father tell you this morning?" she asked. Apparently the story had been fully relayed to her.

Through a flood of tears I answered. "The floors were just waxed and to stay away from there."

My mother just stood there and shook her head. That compassion that I knew resided in her, at that moment seemed to have been trumped by anger, showing itself in her eyes. "Oh, Monique, what am I going to do with you?"

My mother helped me to get out of the family friend's car. Still on skates, I rolled over to my mother's car, crying from the excruciating pain I was in. She lost it when she saw, for the first time, that one of my arms was shaped like the letter S. It looked deformed. She drove me to the hospital where we found out that both my arms were broken as a result of the fall.

I didn't want to see my dad that evening, but he met me and my mom at the hospital. My arms were now in full casts. When our eyes met, I could see the disappointment in his. I had disobeyed my father—done the wrong thing—and now I was paying the price.

My entire summer went by without me being able to ride my bike, skate, build castles on the beach or just plain ole enjoy the outside. It was like being a small, helpless child all over again.

My mother had to bathe me and change my clothes while my father helped to feed me. From that situation, I learned to listen to my parents. My parents have not led me wrong and I've avoided many mistakes by listening to their wisdom. I'm not saying that I'm perfect; far from it. But I have been

able to experience more good than bad.

Chapter 8
Playing Games in My Own Head

My German Sheppard, Coco, lay comfortably in the front yard watching my every move. I was back to my old antics, which were usually not the antics of the average fifteen year old.

I had just learned about an American daredevil and entertainer nicknamed Evel Knievel. I was going to be just like him. With Coco at full attention, I went on a hunt for my father's construction materials to build a volcano ramp. Within thirty minutes, I gathered my father's construction boards, two cinderblocks and other important materials to build my ramp. Coco would raise her head and bark when I struggled with my materials. In my mind, she was encouraging me. I was going to be the female Evel Knievel!

Constructing the volcano ramp took some time, but I was more than pleased when it was complete. I stood still for a while and marveled at my creation. Two complete boards; one in front of the other with five feet between the top of each ramp. This was going to be the greatest daredevil stunt that any teenage country girl had ever done. To pull this off, I needed to be creative.

I quickly ran inside, went to my bedroom and grabbed my skates. "Hey, Mom," I said as I zoomed past her in the kitchen with skates in hand, headed back outdoors.

"Hi, Monique."

Once again outside, I threw my skates in the grass and pulled my yellow ten speed bike from the family bike stand on the side of the house. This was going to be absolutely amazing.

I sat next to Coco and put on my skates. She would be the only front row witness to my glorious stunt . . . Or so I thought.

I had it all planned out in my head. I was going to ride my bike up to the top of the volcano. When airborne, I would let go of the bike and skate down the other side.

The bicycle pedals fit snug between the four wheels of my skates. I started from as far back as possible. I was going to need to work up a lot of speed through the grass to get airborne.

"Are you ready, Coco?" I yelled.

"Woof, woof, woof!"

"Here I go!"

I pressed my left skate deep into the bike pedal. I pressed my right skate into the other. I lifted my backside off the seat and dug even deeper to increase the intensity and speed of my ride. I felt an intense adrenaline rush as I neared the beginning of my volcano ramp. Soon I was on the ramp and on my way to the top. My heart raced.

"CRACK!"

I felt my body rise from my bike and crash onto the ground below.

I landed directly inside my handmade volcano. I couldn't move. I could hear Coco's frantic bark. I began to moan. My body ached all over. I wished Coco would stop barking. I wanted to make sure I succeeded, and therefore I needed to get myself together to take another stab at it. But all of Coco's barking was sure to get my parents' attention, which would more than likely put a halt to the second attempt at my stunt.

I managed to roll to my side. The pain was excruciating.

Unbeknownst to me, my mother had stood in the open kitchen window taking in the show. After a few moments I heard her call out to my father.

"Honey," she yelled. "Your daughter is up to her tricks again! You may want to go out and check on her."

My father ran past my mother through the kitchen and to my rescue. My mother, who was used to my craziness, never let me shake her nerves. She remained in the kitchen preparing dinner. She watched as my father tossed the construction boards from my ailing body. By then, I had managed to sit up on my own. My father picked me up from the ground. I was shaken to say the least.

"Are you all right, Sweetheart?" my father asked.

That question, hearing his voice, brought me back to reality. "Daddy, did I make it? Did I look like Evel Knievel?"

"Baby girl, you were awesome and that's why you're my champ!"

My father kissed me on the forehead and carried me into our home. No, the stunt hadn't ended in the way I had set out for it to end, but never once did my father make me feel as though I had failed. Nor did he discourage me from trying again.

Unfortunately, I had several relatives that tried very hard to get in my head and instill thoughts of failure being an option. Instead of speaking positivity and life into me, they spoke negativity. As a kid it hurt me to know that I had family members that wouldn't encourage me. My parents taught me differently and sometimes it was hard to separate if failure was good or bad. My mom never wanted to see me get hurt, especially with all the physical shenanigans I would engage in. But she knew that I wanted to try everything that I imagined.

As a kid, I experienced two relatives in particular try their best to discourage me, treat me differently, and exclude me because I was dark skinned. I actually overheard a conversation between them regarding my skin color. As young as ten, I realized what was going on and always took the liberty to include myself in activities that they were doing that I wanted to participate in. If I heard a few cousins say they were going to the park and those certain relatives didn't ask me if I wanted to go, I would ask my dad in front of the adults for permission to join as though they had extended an invitation to me. Of course, they would include me then.

It was a lot of work as a kid on my part. I didn't tell my parents what was going on because I didn't want them to be upset and cause any family strife. Family was and still is everything for us. This is why I tried so hard to handle things in a kid way. But I made it a point to never isolate myself around those particular relatives; never knew what they might do. I always stayed around them in a group setting.

I did eventually confront these relatives once I became of legal age. I addressed them each one on one in a very respectful and diplomatic manner.

My parents have always supported me and encouraged me to do things I wanted to do regardless of what society had to say about it. As an adult, I take risk, and if I don't succeed the first time, I continue to try until I do. I don't plan to fail, I plan to succeed. Sometimes it may not be easy, but I stay with it. I generally find a mentor to coach me, one that has successfully done whatever it is that I'm looking to do. I have mentors all over the world now, and I'm not afraid to ask for help. I realize that people are people and I have to be my work-in-progress self, live my life to the fullest, and know that I'm beautiful both inside and out.

Chapter 9
The Educators

Day by day, year by year, the educators of the world commit their lives to educating, preparing, and empowering young people all over the world. These special people enable and encourage, equip and inspire. Throughout the years, many educators have made a major impact in my life. Thoughts of these educators bring up vivid memories. Some of those people stand out a bit more than others. Ms. Rahn, one of my elementary school teachers, is one of those special people.

Ms. Rahn taught me how to communicate effectively. I have always been a big talker, ever since the very early age of five. I could talk all day and all night. I even talked in my sleep, as I was always teased by my mother. One day after one of my extensive rants, Ms. Rahn said to me, "I am going to teach you how to communicate effectively and get your point across to everyone that you meet." Ms. Rahn did just that. The first thing she did was teach me to "slow down."

"No one is going to know what you are talking about if you don't take a breath in between sentences, Monique," she told me. "State your case clearly and concisely and give evidence why your way is the best way," she continued. "Don't expect anyone to just take your word for it." Then she told me something really important. "Once you have stated your case and provided evidence to support it, you have got to know when to stop talking. No one wants something shoved down their throats, and they definitely don't like a know-it-all." Her final word of advice was, "Be careful with your words. Always strive to be honest and sincere, because words are powerful."

Her advice really helped when I wanted to ask for something from my parents. I truly thank her because now I can say that I, too, can communicate effectively.

Facing reality was something that I was taught to do at a young age. I learned that lesson from Mrs. Brown. I was intimidated by Mrs. Brown. She had a reputation for being a strict, no-nonsense teacher. She had been teaching for years. Several of my cousins and one of my aunts had been her students. The first day that I entered her 7th grade classroom, I walked straight to the back of the room and took a seat. I thought that would make me invisible. In the back of the room I could hide and not be called upon or have to talk to Mrs. Brown. One day toward the end of class, the invisible section of the room must have come to light. Mrs. Brown called upon me to answer not one, but two questions. I could have frozen right there in my seat. Needless to say, I answered both questions incorrectly.

Mrs. Brown seemed confused. She looked at the blackboard, looked at me, and then asked, "Monique, can you read the board?" She pointed to a bunch of blurred words she had written on the blackboard. "The answers are written right here."

There were a couple chuckles throughout the room. Talk about the answer being right in front of my face.

I shook my head. "No, ma'am," I answered.

It wasn't that I couldn't see the board; I couldn't *read* what was on the board. I needed glasses. I was too afraid to tell anyone because I didn't want to be called four-eyes or any of the other cruel names that the kids with glasses were called.

Mrs. Brown encouraged me to face the reality that if I was going to do well in school, I needed to be able to see the information being presented to me. Shortly thereafter, I asked my mother if we could take a road trip to the eye doctor in Gainesville, Florida to take care of business. At my appointment I was asked to look into a big machine where there were several rows of letters. The first rows were easy to read. R L M Q T . . . O

F D U K . . . S P N A F . . . Then everything became fuzzy. The doctor confirmed that my vision was off. I was nearsighted and I definitely needed glasses.

I picked out a fancy pair of glasses that looked similar to the ones I saw the pretty news reporter on Channel 12 wear. I loved them and I wasn't teased at all. In fact, most of my peers told me that the glasses made me look smart. I was grateful for Mrs. Brown having a hand in making me face a reality that could have hindered my education otherwise.

Mrs. Williams, another one of my middle school educators, was very different and a bit over the top with making sure that her students followed the rules every second of the day. Most of the students at my school didn't care much for her. My cousin Renee and I became very close with Mrs. Williams and would sometimes go visit her over the weekends. Renee and I met a lot of new friends in Mrs. Williams' neighborhood in Gainesville. When Mrs. Williams was pregnant, she even requested that I name her daughter. I remember giving her a list of names for her and her husband to take a look at and choose from.

She was very challenging and had a very challenging personality. Being a student in her class taught me how to deal with difficult situations.

Leaving home and going away to college was a challenge of its own. It became especially difficult when I learned that a young lady that I had only met once didn't like me, and in fact wanted to fight me. This was very hard for me to understand because I was taught by my parents to love and be kind to everyone. However, day after day, people would tell me that this particular girl from the New York area had no desire to be my friend.

One day I decided that I would face this person and find out why she felt the way she did about me. I decided to talk with her after lunch, even though my other peers pleaded with me not to approach this person.

"No, Monique, don't talk to her. She wants to beat you up," they exclaimed, more fearful of my safety than I was.

As the lunch crowd grew, I boldly approached the young lady. "I need to ask you a question," I said to her.

The crowd began to circle the two of us. Everyone expected to see a fight. However, I was not going to let that happen. Ms. Rahn had taught me how to communicate effectively. I also knew how to deal with challenging personalities thanks to Mrs. Williams.

"I understand that you have a problem with me," I stated with a smile.

"Yes, I don't like you," she replied.

"How can you say that you don't like me when we've only known each other for a week?" I asked.

"I don't like you because you smile all the time," she stated.

"That's the problem?" I innocently asked. "I can tell you why I smile all the time. My father spent a lot of money on my dental work. He told me afterward that he always wanted me to smile."

My potential enemy looked confused.

"Now that you have an answer, can we just be friends?" I extended my right hand to hers.

She shook my hand. Since everyone was around waiting and watching, I wanted them to know that we all were going to be friends. I knew that I was in control of my personality and that particular situation. I then turned to everyone and said, "Now that she and I are friends, we are all going to have a big group hug!" So the fight that everyone expected to see turned into a great situation. All of us became good friends.

I can't forget about Mrs. Moore. She was one of my high school educators who taught me how to study. One day she was returning papers that our class had done. I looked at my grade and compared it with my peers' seated around me. I raised my hand and was called upon by Mrs. Moore.

"I need to know why I received a B and everyone else received an A," I inquired.

"Well, Monique, you did not earn an A," she replied.

My feelings were hurt. I hung my head throughout the remainder of class. As the bell rang, I gathered my belongings and began to leave the classroom.

Mrs. Moore must have realized the impact that her response had on me, because she met me at the door. "Let's talk," she said. "Apparently you are having some difficulties with this course work that we need to deal with. So I'm going to teach you how to study."

That day, I stayed with Mrs. Moore after class. I also put in a few more hours of studying and met with Mrs. Moore again later that week. I realized that I had been copying the study habits of my sister, who was a straight A student. She was very smart and didn't have to put forth a lot of effort in studying at home, yet was still able to be very successful in the classroom. In addition to making superb grades, my sister would take the hardest classes; the advanced courses. Upon seeing my sister's classroom success, I began to think that if I took easier classes, I could make all A's as well.

Mrs. Moore told me that it wasn't about taking an easier class. She explained that I would still need to learn how to study and that she would continue to teach me how to do so.

I took Mrs. Moore's advice and stayed in her class although I thought it was very hard. A few weeks later, Mrs. Moore moved about the classroom handing back the papers that our class had completed. She put my paper face down on my desk. I reluctantly flipped the paper over to see what grade I had earned. Upon seeing the grade, a great, big smile appeared on my face. I had received my first A in that class. I now knew how to study and Mrs. Moore helped me gain patience with myself through that learning process.

Mr. McGriff, another one of my high school educators, was the teacher who encouraged me to become the best me.

"I want you to stop comparing yourself to your siblings," he said. "Your siblings are both athletic and your sister makes really good grades without having to do much studying. You are you, Monique."

He told me to become the person that I dreamed of becoming and not the person that someone expected me to become.

Mrs. Stephens, my accounting instructor, one day realized that I had no desire to be in her class. Every day I would go into class unprepared and basically sit for the whole time doing other work, or just staring out the window. On this particular day, I was really focused on the football game taking place later that evening. She said to me, "Wherever you go in life, you are going to have to manage your money or someone else's money. You really need to focus on this class." Mrs. Stephens further reiterated the fact that money management was very important. I took heed to her words and began to focus on that class . . . And it paid off.

Several years ago I ran into Coach Karen and Coach Tommy, two of my post college influences. These two people taught me how to train and run or walk marathons. I was never athletic as a kid, a teenager, or in undergraduate school. I learned then that I still could be athletic today. After training with them for five and a half months, I was able to run a 26.2 mile marathon. I finished! I made it to the end. And when I finished, I said, "Lessons learned!"

Today, I can honestly say that I am athletic and I completed my Master's degree. I, too, now have a balance. I can relate to my siblings who were all intelligent, driven and wonderful athletes as well. I have now arrived! It took hard work, dedication and consistent prayer to get me to the finish line, to study and to make very good grades in grad school. Life is good, especially when you are living as the very best you!

Chapter 10
Right On! Magazine

As a new high school freshman, I came up with a wonderful, innovative way to meet new and exciting teenagers from all over the world. I loved music, visiting different beaches, water sports, and four wheeling in the mud. I was interested in meeting other teens who shared the same hobbies. I wanted to know what was going on with teens outside of my area; what was going on at their high school? What kind of extracurricular activities did they participate in? What was their school mascot? I had a million questions that I needed answers to and I was determined to find out.

During that time, *Right On!* Magazine was all the rage. If you wanted to know what was going on in the world of teenagers and what was hip, you read *Right On!* So naturally, I asked Mom if I could take out a subscription. After she took a look through the magazine, she agreed that it was suitable. I was so excited because there was something in the back of the magazine that I knew would help me reach my goal of meeting other teens.

The next morning as my mom headed out to work, she went to the dining room and picked up all the outgoing mail off the table. We lived in a rural area and did not have a mailbox, so all of our mail came and went through the post office. It was a family practice to leave all mail or packages that needed to be sent out on the dining room table, that way Mom could mail them on her way to work. I had placed my magazine subscription order on the table the night before and couldn't wait until I received my first magazine in the mail.

Four weeks went by and I had gotten into the habit of waking up and checking my dresser first thing in the morning for mail . . . And then being disappointed. I was just starting to get impatient when my first copy of *Right On!* arrived. I opened it up and went to sit on the front porch swing. I was so totally engrossed in my magazine that I didn't even realize my sister, Lisa, and cousin, Renee, were standing over me laughing.

"Gosh, Monique," Lisa said. "You are glued to that magazine like Elmer's!"

I glanced up as Lisa and Renee shared a laugh. "It's a lot of great things in here," I said to them. "Look at this." I pointed to the back page where the pen pal page was.

Lisa looked at the page and said, "Girl, I don't care about no pen pals. I just want to know about the cute guys." She laughed, giving Renee a high-five.

I looked at both of them. "Well, I want to meet new people from all over the world, and if Mom lets me place an ad, I'll bet some of my pen pals will probably be cute guys too!" I went back to looking at all of the names on the page.

"Well, Monique, when you do get some pen pals-" Renee started.

"You mean if Mom let's her," Lisa interrupted.

"Yeah, if Auntie lets you get pen pals, let us know if any of them are cute guys," Renee finished as she and Lisa went into the house.

I sat there fantasizing about meeting new friends all afternoon, and when my mom came home from work, I showed her the pen pal page and asked if I could place my own ad. She looked at a couple of the ads and told me she would let me do it, but she would monitor all of my letters closely because there were some dangerous people in the world.

I was so happy when I sat down to fill out the questionnaire asking what kind of teenage friends I was looking for. As soon as I was done, I ran into the dining room and put my mail on the table. After that I went into my room and decorated a cute little "mail basket" to put on my dresser for all of my mail, because I was confident I would receive a lot!

It took almost two months before my first correspondence came. Lisa and Renee were also excited and couldn't wait until I received pictures from some cute guys. The first batch of mail contained three letters for me, and I received at least one letter a day for the rest of the month. Every time Mom went to the post office, I had at least five letters. For the first three months I received anywhere from 30 to 50 letters a week. I felt like I was a celebrity.

Keeping up with the incoming letters was hard to do, and I was so busy that I was unable to respond to all of them in a day. Evidently, the post office was having difficulty with my newfound celebrity status as well, because a couple of times Mom would find a note in the box to come to the counter because there was too much mail to fit into our box.

At home I was using pillow cases to store all of my mail. I was so busy reading and writing letters that I had little time for anything else. I would soon require additional hands.

One Saturday I called some of my cousins in Jacksonville and asked if they could come and help me sort through my mountain of pen pal letters.

They jumped at the chance. Soon after they arrived, we had set up a system that organized the letters by state. After we organized them, Mom came in and started scanning through the piles. Before long she noticed a pattern with number codes on the return addresses. Remarkably, I was receiving pen pal requests from teenage prisoners; some who were locked up for life! Those letters were some of the more interesting ones I'd received.

In one letter a 19 year old told me he was serving a 10 year sentence. His father was in the same prison serving life PLUS ten years, and if he lived he could get out the first Monday after Easter the following year.

I was confused; I had never heard of such a thing. Needless to say, Mom did not allow me to write him back. But I had to admit, his letter was very interesting.

Through *Right On!* Magazine, I was able to meet so many new friends. Many are lifelong friends that I still have to this day. Sad to say, the best friend I made through my pen pal experiment died from AIDS complications. Her husband had an affair with a person he described as "the most beautiful woman he had ever laid eyes on." Too bad he was looking at the outer packaging and didn't think to protect his family better, because he lost his wife, then he died six months later; leaving three children without parents.

Another great pen pal I met inspired me to perform community service. We talked about doing meaningful things in the world and eventually we began meeting up and doing some of the things we had talked about. A few years after we met, we started going to visit the elderly and the sick and shut in. We would do the women's hair, polish their nails and moisturize and rub their feet. We were also able to get some of the male pen pals to do the same with men. As I said before, some of my pen pals were great people who went on to do great things.

I had quite a few who went on to play college and professional sports, so I was able to attend a few games for free. I also had a pen pal from Paris who would send me the most beautiful postcards. I never did meet her in person, but thankfully I was able to visit Paris, France some years later.

I had a nice pen pal from Bermuda who had family living in Idaho. She was able to visit the United States and purchase her own copy of *Right On!* Magazine. She would send me pretty pictures of her beautiful surroundings. I have since visited Bermuda to run a marathon with Georgia

Team in Training, and I must say the pictures were pretty accurate. Bermuda is breathtaking!

Because of my pen pals, I was able to go to a lot of different school sporting events with free tickets. I went to Disneyland in California for a pen pal's birthday party. Thankfully her mom was a flight attendant and my ticket was of no cost. I even attended a NASCAR event at no charge, compliments of a pen pal. I was super excited because I was able to meet professional race car drivers.

I really enjoyed my visit with pen pal friends to the Apollo Theater in Harlem and Mackinac Island in Michigan. We had a blast! I had the opportunity to eat at Roscoe's Chicken and Waffles in California, and I have to admit, breakfast and lunch work well together. And most amazingly, I was able to attend an NBA Draft and an NBA Draft party for a pen pal's cousin. Shoot, I attended my first Atlanta Braves baseball game compliments of a pen pal.

I think the pen pal experiment was one of my greatest ideas. I immensely enjoyed receiving all those letters, and as much work as it was, I enjoyed writing them back. I made a lot of great friends who helped me reach my Girl Scout 100 cookie goal every year, so that was a definite plus.

It was a joy to share my world and have them share theirs. I learned a lot and made great memories over the years. In fact, I received pen pal letters until the end of my freshman year in college. Each time I received one, I would smile because it was such an amazing experience.

I thank God for providing me with the opportunity to meet and communicate with all those hundreds of creative, kind, interesting teens; some who turned out to be influential, inspirational adults. Most of all, I thank *Right On!* Magazine for their ingenious idea to include the pen pal section. For a curious, adventurous, young girl, it was indeed *Right On!* time…

Chapter 11
Never Sprint . . . Instead, Run a Marathon

As far back as I can remember, my parents spent a lot of time and money supporting my little brother, Big D, and his dreams of being a professional athlete. As a little girl, I would ride shotgun while my mother chauffeured my brother and all of his little friends from one sporting event to another; including little league football, basketball, and baseball. I was only two years older than my brother, but I was always the doting big sister and very protective of him. I always behaved older than my years, so I was the "little mama" and his fierce protector.

I used to turn around in my seat to make sure all the boys were wearing their seatbelts. I would get a good laugh looking at them in their baseball gear. They were so little and their feet didn't even touch the floor. They would just sit there dangling their legs back and forth, and I thought they were the cutest little guys ever!

With all of his training, it was no surprise that Big D was always the first one chosen to be on a team when it came to sports. While I was not athletic at all, I was my brother's number one fan. I fully supported his athletic endeavors and made it a point to be at all of his games. In fact, my parents and entire family spent countless hours in the stands cheering him on to victory.

Mom and Dad were fully committed to making sure Big D had every opportunity to pursue athletics. They offered unwavering support, both emotionally and financially. It was the consensus that Big D would be the one to make it big in sports. We all knew the sky was the limit for him as long as he kept his grades up and stayed on the straight and narrow, which didn't seem to be a problem for my handsome, charismatic little brother.

Once he reached high school, Big D was the man! He was six feet, six inches of fine chocolate with basketball skills to match; hence the name Big D. My little brother was no longer so little, and he had the whole world at his fingertips; a promising future in basketball, a family who loved and supported him, and a community of fans who thought the sun rose and set on him. But he took it all for granted.

"What are you doing?" I asked my brother as he blew out a puff of marijuana smoke. I had I rode up on him on my ten speed bicycle. He sat, with the window down, on the passenger side of my uncle's car that was parked on a side street near the high school gym.

Big D looked at me and sucked his teeth before turning away.

I looked over at my uncle, who was planted in the driver's seat. I stared at him with disappointment before once again confronting my brother. "Are you crazy?" I asked.

Big D turned to face me with a frown on his face. "Quit making a big deal out of everything. Dang! It's not like I'm an addict or anything. It's just a little bit of weed, Mo," he replied. "You always blowing things out of proportion."

I placed both hands on my hips because I wanted him to know I was serious. "D, if you don't stop, I promise I will tell Mom and Dad," I threatened. "You don't need to be smoking that mess, and I'm not blowing anything out of proportion! You are my little brother and I am supposed to look out for you."

He shook his head and looked over at my uncle. They shared a laugh and my brother shrugged his shoulders.

"Go ahead and tell," Big D said as my uncle started the car and drove off, leaving me there full of anger and disappointment.

For days I contemplated telling my parents what I had witnessed. I was so scared for my brother. I spent moments alternating between being angry at my uncle and being disappointed that my brother would risk his whole future for a few puffs of pleasure. I was confused and I did not understand how my uncle could expose his young nephew to illegal drugs. I felt like he should have been ashamed of himself. Didn't he realize Big D's potential? Didn't he understand the risks that were involved? What if Big D became addicted? All of these questions bounced around inside of my head day after day. But remarkably, neither my uncle nor my brother seemed to care. For them it was "business as usual."

"Yo, Big D, you played a good game, man!" my cousin yelled from across the gym.

"Thanks, man. I'll see you in a little bit," Big D called back as he went into the locker room. With 32 points and 13 rebounds to his credit, Big D had brought his A game once again and was headed out to celebrate with the fellas.

I hung around the locker room door waiting for him. I was hoping to convince him to hang out with me like we used to, but I was skeptical. Over the past year my brother had developed a bad habit and was smoking weed quite often. While I had tried to talk to him and discourage him from smoking, it was all in vain. My charismatic, talented, handsome brother was addicted.

"Girl, get out of my face," Big D said as he walked out of the locker room. "Stop following me and mind your own business," he spat out as he quickly walked toward the exit.

"I'm just trying to help," I began as I tried to keep up with him.

All of a sudden he stopped abruptly, turned around and looked down at me. "I don't want your help and I don't need your help. You live in your own little, happy bubble and have no clue about my life, so stop trying to tell me what I should and shouldn't be doing. Pleeease, just LEAVE ME ALONE!" he said before walking away to join his friends.

I left the gymnasium feeling like the weight of the world was on my shoulders. My feelings were hurt because I knew the old Big D would've never spoken to me like that. I had already tried talking to his friends and a few family members, but no one saw his smoking as a problem. If they even believed me, all they had to say was that I was overreacting and assured me that it was a phase that he would get past. Needless to say, I wasn't so sure of that. I had a sinking feeling deep down in my gut that things would only get worse. But how do you tell a family that their idol might be a little tarnished?

I went home that night and pulled out my diary. It seemed that writing was the only way I could find some relief from worrying about my brother. I poured out my heartbreak on paper, writing about how hard it was watching Big D destroy himself day after day. Some nights I would leave my diary wide open on the living room floor, praying that someone would read it and I would not be alone in my worries, but no one ever did.

Mom would find it and just put it on my dresser while I slept. Daddy had expressed on more than one occasion that my diary was my own private thoughts and NO ONE should ever be caught reading it. So I guess my prayers were in vain.

While no one else could see it, I had begun noticing subtle changes in Big D's appearance and behavior. He was, after all, my little brother. I watched him grow up and develop into a young man. I knew him well and could tell his drug use had begun to take a toll on him. Sadly, I was the only one who seemed to notice or even care.

As the years went on, Big D continued with his drug use, but remarkably, he still managed to dominate on the basketball court. While he did falter a bit in the classroom, he was given the opportunity to attend summer school to make up his credits. As you can imagine, I had taken on the role of Big D's shadow and I followed him everywhere I could, even summer school. Of course he was very unhappy with me. He told me I was "out of touch" and he called me a nuisance, but nevertheless, I continued my shadow routine, to no avail. He never stopped smoking, in fact, things got progressively worse.

"How does he do it?" I wondered out loud while watching Big D control the basketball court like a professional. His drug use had started to show on his face, but when he took to the court, he was a beast! He was a superstar ball player with a promising future. That's what everyone saw when they looked at him; a number one college prospect. Seemingly, I was the only one who saw his life spiraling out of control.

Big D ended up with a basketball scholarship to play Division 1 basketball at Tennessee. Even though he was in another state, I continued fighting for my brother's life. Oftentimes I would make the drive from Atlanta to Tennessee to watch him play. I always made the effort to speak to all the police officers and important people on campus. I wanted to make sure they knew who I was, so that if anything ever went down with my brother, they would know who to call. I would walk right up to the police officers, extend my hand and introduce myself. I never disclosed my true intentions, but I wanted them to remember me . . . Just in case. And amazingly, they did.

I started being given special privileges like preferred parking and super good seats to all the games. As great as this was, it still didn't change the fact that my brother had yet to acknowledge his issue with drugs. But soon he would have to face his problem.

It was after midnight on a Friday night when I received the phone call that made me jump out of bed and drive through the night to Tennessee. One of my contacts had let me know that my brother was acting out of character at a party, and they were worried. In my mind, I actually thought I was going to get Big D under control. In retrospect, I see now I was just fooling myself.

When I arrived, it was obvious that my brother was under the influence. Thinking it was going to make a difference, I tried talking to him, but in the mental state he was in, I was basically a gnat buzzing around his head. He did not hear one word I was saying. I had to admit I wasn't able to control or influence his behavior. I left the party no closer to helping him than I had been in Atlanta. I rode around and found a place to park my car and fell asleep, determined to get up the next morning and have a heart to heart talk with my brother.

The next morning, I looked at my surroundings and realized the magnitude of the situation. Here I was hundreds of miles away from home, sleeping in a parking lot with a bag of snacks, two bottles of water and a bottle of fruit punch PowerAde—trying to save someone who didn't think he needed to be saved. Nevertheless, I had driven all of this way and I was not leaving until he heard me out.

I reached into my gym bag and pulled out one of my workout towels and a bottle of water. I "brushed my teeth" as best as I could and washed my face, then drove to Big D's dorm.

Knocking on the door I felt a little bit of nervous anxiety. I wondered in what condition I would find Big D and would he finally listen to reason. He opened the door and looked at me and said, "It's you again."

Big D was surrounded by his basketball players. The majority of them were acting out just as he was. For some, they were worse off than he was. The difference between them and my brother was that Big D had a family that cared about him and were not just willing to let him fall by the wayside, even when he was mean. Nevertheless, those three words, and the distain in his tone when he said them, cut to my core. My feelings were so hurt because when did I become "you again?" I was his sister who happened to love him dearly. I wasn't some stranger off the street who was just there to mind his business. But I sucked up my hurt feelings and asked him to come down to the activity room to talk to me. Reluctantly he did.

As he leaned against the wall, I could see that my brother was tormented. He seemed very unhappy, and not just because I was there pestering him. There was more to it. I asked him what was really going on and what was so wrong with his life that he felt the need to abuse drugs and get drunk. He complained about his coach getting on his nerves and a couple of other minor issues, but I could see that they were all just excuses. I told him if he could get himself together, in two years he would be playing in the NBA making more money than his coach would see in a lifetime. Most importantly, I told him that he would be doing what he loved most in the world; playing basketball. I also let him know that his other option was to stay on the same track and deal with the consequences of his actions. It was up to him.

"Big D, I just want to help you. I love you," I pleaded near tears. "What can I do to help you?"

He turned away from me and began to walk away. "You can just leave me alone," he replied and left me standing there in the midst of my turmoil.

I drove home deep in thought, telling myself that I had done the best that I could. I got home and drew a bubble bath to try and relax. I laid there and thought about all that I had tried to do. I wondered what else I could have done. It was with that thought that I arose from the tub, got dressed and got down on my knees and prayed.

After my prayer, I got a second wind and decided to drive to Florida and have a heart to heart talk with my parents. I prayed they would be ready to receive all that I had to share. I especially worried about how my mother would take the news. It was not going to be easy talking to her about her son. Needless to say, they were not ready to hear the truth, and with my feelings hurt once again, I left Florida after an overnight stay.

A few months later things went downhill for my brother and my parents had no option but to recognize the seriousness of his problem. They sought help for him, and for a while things got better, but his life continued to be a rollercoaster of highs and lows. He would go through a recovery period and then he would backslide. This went on for well over ten years.

Though it hurt my family, my mother had a steadfast, no nonsense rule that she refused to break, even for her beloved son. My mother refused to let anyone, family or otherwise, come into her home and disrespect it. Needless to say, my brother has not been home for a visit since the late 1990s.

Over the last six years, we have had family dinners and continue to visit with my brother in Georgia, but it's not the same. While we communicate often, I miss the relationship I shared with him, and I continue to pray for him.

I struggled with feeling guilty that I could have done more for my brother. I didn't share that with anyone, though. I now know that I did all I could do. I wanted to save my brother; however, my brother wasn't really willing to save himself. I've learned that it doesn't matter how much you want to save a family member or friend, they must want it more than you. When it's something they want, they'll make it happen.

Over the years I sought ways to heal and move forward from the experience of watching a loved one struggle with an addiction. While I am the least athletic member of the Chandler clan, I decided to take up running. I felt like this would help me to clear my mind and also add another layer to my workout. But I didn't just want to run for that reason; I wanted to make a positive difference in the lives of people who also struggled.

I began researching different running groups and sending out inquiries. I received a response from the Leukemia and Lymphoma team and was delighted that their coaches were willing to train me. We started training two weeks later, and I must admit, I struggled badly and I did more walking than running on my first run. I went home that evening, tired but determined to find a way to motivate me to run and build up my endurance.

I sat down and came up with a plan to purge myself of the things in my life that continued to hold me back. I took out a sheet of paper and began writing down the things in my life that I needed to resolve. By the time I was finished, I had written down 26 of the most painful things that had been a "thorn in my side." My page was full of hurt from things that my brother had taken me and my family through, as well as a few other things. I had so much pent up anger and frustration that I had pushed to the back of my mind, it surprised me how well I had been able to cover up my pain. But through this outlet, I was determined that now was the time for release.

I trained very hard, and each time I set out to run, I thought of all the hurt and pain I had gone through. Before long, I began to see a shift in my body. It looked amazing, but there was still the presence of hurt and pain in my heart. People would offer me the most heartfelt compliments on my appearance, never knowing of the deep seeded pain I harbored on the inside. But I would soon be blessed with an opportunity to release it all through a great opportunity to bless someone else.

My run team flew to California to run for a young child in Georgia who had been diagnosed with Leukemia. My heart went out because this child never had the opportunity to play basketball because of the restless nights of chemo. I thought about the opportunities my brother had and the fact that he took his opportunities for granted. Even after all that he had been through, Big D had still been given the opportunity to go and tryout for two NBA teams, but his priority had been partying instead of practicing. So once again, yet another opportunity slipped through his fingers. I made the decision to move on from that, once again having to come to grips with why I was so desperate to save someone who didn't want to be saved.

Race day dawned beautiful and full of possibilities, but the only thing I thought about was completing the race. All I wanted to do was finish, but 26.2 miles was looming ahead and I was nervous. Once I reached the start line, I knew in my heart that I would indeed finish.

In the pockets of my shorts I had 26 small pieces of paper that contained my heartbreak, and I was determined to release it all. I was prayed up and ready to go!

At the start of the race, I pulled out the first piece of paper. It read, "Forgive your uncle for introducing your brother to marijuana, and start speaking to him again."

During that first mile, I processed all of my negative feelings toward my uncle, and at the end of the mile, I tossed the paper away. For 26 miles I did this, and one by one, I tossed my pain and heartbreak by the wayside. By the time I reached the finish line, I felt like a new person.

My first marathon medal means more to me than the hard work I put in training for it. It represents the compassion in my heart I had for that child in need. More than anything, it represents my growth as a person and a child of God, with the capacity to forgive and love unconditionally.

Chapter 12
Family Resources

I'm a country girl; a down home, barefoot, country roads take me home, daydreaming, sometimes tomboy and other times girlie-girl kind of girl. I'm proud of the place I call home. My childhood home sits nestled in the backwoods of a small town in Florida, away from all the hustle and bustle of city life. It's a quiet, peaceful existence, full of nature's own creations; lush green grass and trees for miles around . . . And I love it! I was raised in the country with nearby horses, pigs, cows, and chickens. When I wasn't in school, I had plenty of fun activities to keep me busy.

After completing my homework, three days a week I cleaned and tended to my uncle Ancil's rabbits, all the while daydreaming. At night I was either lost between the pages of a good travel book, or floating in my own private utopia, excitedly scribbling in my diary about the many adventures I would take once I reached adulthood and could afford to travel on my own.

Reading afforded me the opportunity to travel and see distant lands in my mind, and I was blessed with an imagination vivid enough to dream in color. But eventually that was no longer enough. I wanted to see the world for myself; witness its wonders through my own eyes and touch the magnificence with my own hands. I would not be satisfied until I was able to hear nature's beautiful sounds with my own ears, and smell the fresh air and taste the different cuisines from one end of the country to the other. I wanted to use all five of my senses to do it all!

My family and I traveled every now and then, but in my book, going to funerals didn't count as an adventure. I never got a chance to explore the places we visited; just got dressed, attended services, ate dinner and hit the road. I was a young girl with bright eyes and big ideas; curious about the world. I was tired of just reading about these wondrous places. I wanted to *experience* these wondrous places. I wanted to climb the Great Smoky Mountains and view the world from way up high, dip my feet in the Pacific Ocean, see the Grand Canyon, visit the casinos in Vegas and make snow angels in the Upper Peninsula of Michigan. What about hang gliding and roller skating on the Santa Monica Pier? I wanted to do it all, and the sooner my bags were packed and I was on my way, the better.

The summer before my senior year in high school, I decided that I wanted to visit *every* state in the United States. I dreamed about how much fun I would have and all the different people I would meet on my journey.

It gave me such an indescribable feeling on the inside when I would imagine dining in fine restaurants and even little hole in the wall eateries. I dreamed that I would travel to historic Savannah, Georgia and eat seafood on the riverfront. My mouth would literally tingle when I thought about eating authentic Cajun food on Bourbon Street, and I couldn't wait to enjoy a huge slice of New York pizza in the big apple. I could feel the cheese dripping down my chin and taste the spices on my tongue. Yes! I was definitely going to find a way to make my dreams into reality, but I had no job that would afford me the money needed, and no resources. So the odds of me reaching this goal were not in my favor. I thought about it over and over, and at night, in between reading and writing, I prayed for God to make a way to bring everything into fruition.

"Momma and Daddy, I need your help," I said as I walked into the living room one Monday evening. Daddy was reading the newspaper and Mom was sitting on the couch engrossed in an episode of *Let's Make a Deal*. Before either of them could respond, I launched into my spiel. "I know this sounds crazy, but I really, really, really want to travel," I gushed with teenage enthusiasm.

I could see my mom's left eyebrow raise slightly, giving me the I-beg-your-pardon look. Daddy's newspaper rattled a bit and he cleared his throat, letting me know I had his attention.

I decided to dive right in. "Before you answer, can you please just promise me you will think about it before you say no? I mean, I know I don't have any money, but I promise you I will come up with something." I paused to think. "Or you all can help me." I drew in a deep breath as an idea formed in my head. "I'm so excited," I squealed as I turned and rushed out of the room, leaving my parents in stunned silence.

A few days later, before approaching my parents again, I laid out a map on the dining room table, along with my diary that was full of ideas. "Momma and Daddy," I yelled, immediately apologizing to my daddy because we were not allowed to raise our voice in the house. "Can you come in here, please?"

When they both walked into the room, I could see a cautious look on my mom's face as she surveyed the map on the table. "Um, what is this for?" she asked, looking at me inquisitively.

Daddy just took his seat at the table, trying hard to hide the amused twinkle that I saw light up his eyes.

"Well, I've been thinking," I started as I opened up my diary.

Mom sat down and put her elbows on the table, resting her face in both hands and stared at me wide-eyed.

"I've decided that I want to visit every state in the United States," I said proudly.

Mom made a move to speak, but I continued on before she could get out a word.

"See, the way I figure it, you both have really big families and they are spread all over the U.S., so at least we know that I have family who I can see and maybe stay with while traveling," I said in one quick motion. "See, I've already marked the states I know we have relatives in. That's almost half of the United States already," I pointed out. "Look, Cousin Lewis and his wife are stationed at Fort Leonard Wood, Missouri, Cousin Ariel and her family are stationed at Fort Ord, California, and Cousin Meghan is living at Fort Jackson with her husband. Cousin Brianna is in graduate school and has a condo near the University of Iowa in Iowa City. That will give me a chance to visit a college campus while I am traveling. In fact, according to my notes, I can potentially visit nine college campuses on my journey," I finished with satisfaction. I had a feeling that little tidbit might help my case.

"Let me see what you have, Baby Girl," Daddy said as he shifted in his seat to see the map better. Picking up my red marker on the table, he began marking off other states. "Write this down," he said. "My aunt Sue lives here in Atlantic City, New Jersey." He pointed. "And her daughter, Delia, lives in South Florida. Your first cousin, Freda, lives in Tacoma, Washington. Oh yeah, I have a cousin, Kyle, who lives in Montana."

I looked over at Mom and I could see her interest was piqued.

"What about you, Mom?" I asked. "Do you have any relatives in any of these states? I already have Grandma and Uncle George marked off. I have your twin cousins, Mary and Martha, marked off too. Are they still in Detroit, Michigan?" I asked.

Reluctantly, she reached over and grabbed my diary. "Let me see who you left off," she finally said with resignation in her voice.

By the time we were finished, we had marked off relatives living in 41 states! I was so excited that I didn't know what to do. The plan was for me to write a letter to my family members in which I would introduce myself and tell them about my journey. I asked them to provide housing and food during my stay, and I would provide my own transportation. During each visit I would stay for at least a four day weekend, or as long as a week if there were more relatives in the area who wanted to meet me. I was set! My adventure would begin as soon as I graduated in June.

The day after graduation, I started on my journey, with my first destination being West Palm Beach, Florida. As I rode Greyhound, Trailways and Amtrak throughout Florida, and flew across the country, I grew more and more excited at each new destination. I was able to visit rural areas, farms, desert lands, city streets and barren lands. I mountain biked, golfed, visited museums and got to eat the famous Garrett's Popcorn in Chicago. I excitedly watched the apple drop on New Year's Day in New York, and was finally able to make snow angels in Upper Peninsula, Michigan.

I met so many new family members and was blessed to break bread with them in dining rooms and restaurants all over the country. I went skydiving, bungee jumping, mountain climbing, trail walking, deep sea fishing, and horseback riding. I was totally amazed by the beautiful scenery along the way. There were the astounding mountains in Tennessee and amazing beaches along the East Coast. I was able to go sailing and attended all sorts of professional sporting events. I went to plays on Broadway and attended a boxing match in Las Vegas. I even visited huge churches I had only heard about or had seen on television. I got to visit several of my favorites like Joel Osteen's and even attended church at The Potter's House. It was an absolute joy having the opportunity to hear TD Jakes speak live. And while I didn't go inside, I was able to see Joyce Meyer Ministries on one of my many sightseeing expeditions.

Oh, and did I mention the variety of food? From delicious home cooked meals shared around the dinner table to the yummy New York pizza I had only dreamed about, I went from state to state, cuisine to cuisine. Heck, I became a "foodie" before they even coined the term; sampling fish and grits down in Georgia, delicious Mexican sour cream chicken Enchiladas with black beans and rice cuisine over in Texas, and delicious lobster up in Maine.

After spending so much time traveling, I was able to amass enough frequent flier miles to be able to visit the other nine states where I didn't have family residing, thus attaining my goal of visiting all 50 states.

Perhaps one of the funnier and more memorable experiences occurred in North Dakota. As I shopped in a store for some essentials, I felt a pinch on my leg. I looked down and there was a little blond haired boy staring back up at me with awe in his eyes. His parents stood not far away, also staring—out of embarrassment. The little boy had never seen an African American and he had pinched me to see if I was real. After apologizing profusely, the boy's parents invited me to dinner at a local restaurant where I was able to enjoy yet another delicious meal.

I collected so many mementos and priceless memories during several years spent traveling, that they will forever reside in a special place in my heart. Through this enlightening journey across the United States, I was able to meet extended family and explore more than my young heart could have ever imagined. As a result, I yearned to see more, and thankfully, I have had the opportunity to venture outside of the United States to many countries. Traveling brightens my heart; as I live to travel, but mostly I travel to live!

Chapter 13
Grad Night

It was the spring of my high school senior year and I was preparing for a big night. I excitedly planned my outfit for the next day; meticulously laying out my black dress, multicolored belts and black stockings. I topped off the combination with my high heeled zebra print pumps and a single white glove. Yes, I had my Michael Jackson outfit ready and I already knew how I wanted to style my hair. I was headed to Grad Night at Disney World the next evening, so I was beyond excited!

Grad Night, which is now called Grad Bash, is a full night of fun for high school seniors hosted by Walt Disney World. The information sheet we received at school said the park opened up late in the evening, around 8 p.m., and stayed open until six the next morning. We were going to get to enjoy unlimited rides, attend live concerts, and shop in the Disney store. What I was really looking forward to was hanging out and partying with teenagers from different schools all across the state of Florida. I had lots of cousins in St. Petersburg and Palm Springs, and I was looking forward to seeing my friend, Candice, who was one of the pen pals I met through *Right*

On! Magazine. We had been exchanging letters since 10th grade and were really excited to have the opportunity to hang out.

I was sitting on the bus staring out the window as we pulled up at Disney, watching as busses arrived from every direction. I was in awe. I had never seen so many buses. School buses, chartered buses, and mini vans in every color lined the front gate curb as teenagers from every ethnic background exited the buses and headed for the entrance. I pulled out my compact mirror and checked my reflection one last time to make sure everything was in place. I checked out my teased hair and smiled. "Cyndi Lauper ain't got nothing on me," I said to myself.

I checked my collar to make sure it was standing and that my belts were arranged in order. After that I checked my lip gloss, fluffed my bang one last time, closed the mirror and joined the thousands of seniors at the Disney gate.

The fun began and never seemed to end as we rode many of the rides in the park over and over. We walked around taking pictures with everyone from future Division 1 sports prospects, to folks wearing cool outfits. We had dance offs with students from other schools, and had the opportunity to discuss current events with students that could relate with things going on with our generation. We shared contact information so we all could stay in touch after high school. Many of us were heading to college after high school, and some were going into the Military. A few were headed off to trade schools around the country. We did meet some students that decided moving away from home would be too much and overwhelming, so they planned to live at home and attend a local community college.

Whatever others decided for their lives was fine with me. I was leaving home the morning after high school graduation to start living my own life. My dreams and goals were endless, and I was ready to explore.

"Ooh wait . . . Wait a minute." I breathed out as I sat down on a bench. "My feet are killing me," I whined.

Candice and my cousin Linda looked at each other and shook their heads.

"Mo, I don't know what you were thinking wearing those heels in the first place," Linda said as she took a seat beside me.

We had only been in the park for three and a half hours and I was almost down for the count. We had stood in so many lines that I just wanted to take my shoes off and throw them in the nearest trashcan, but I knew better than that. But in order for me to survive, I had to find a solution, and I mean quick!

"Come on," Candice said. "Let's go find you some flats to put on so we can get to The Dazz Band concert," she said as both she and Linda took me by the elbows and hoisted me up from the bench.

By the time we made it to the nearest store, my shoes were one step closer to the trash can, but instead of tossing them, I took them off, put them in my purse and proceeded to walk around the store until I came across a display of thick, colorful Disney socks with cute little characters on them. I picked up a pair of pink ones with Minnie Mouse on them and quickly walked to the counter. I gave the tag to the cashier as I bent down and put them on. My friends laughed at me, but I didn't care, because those socks felt like heaven on my aching feet.

For the next few hours we watched the many groups perform as we danced the night away. We laughed as Weird Al Yankovic sang his version of Michael Jackson's song, "Beat It," called "Eat It." And of course since I was dressed like Michael, I put on a show; imitating the King of Pop the best way I knew how. By the time The Dazz Band got finish performing, we had "Whipped It" so hard until my hair was whipped too. We danced in the bubbles and smoke and even enjoyed a little bit of Night Ranger and Dwight Tilley before we exhausted ourselves and had to take a break.

Candice, Linda and I managed to find an unoccupied bench and took a seat. I sat there watching the other teenagers walk by, thinking to myself what an awesome night it had been. Oh sure, my body was tired, but there was so much more to see. Beside me, Candice had leaned on Linda's shoulder and was letting out a big yawn. Linda looked like she was going to go down any minute, so I leaned over on Linda's shoulder and took a little nap. After about 30 minutes we woke up and straightened our outfits, fluffed our hair and took off in search of a smoked turkey leg.

By the time the gates opened again at six a.m., I was exhausted! As I hugged all of my friends and more relatives from Miami, Fort Pierce, and Jacksonville, I remember thinking, *Back to Reality.*

While we were inside the park it was easy to believe the fantasy— hanging out, partying and meeting new people—but as soon as I made it back to my seat on the bus, I remembered all the things I had to do when I made it home. I thought about all the tasks I had to complete in order to be ready to move on to the next level. Though my body was tired, my mind was on ten.

When I got back home, instead of sleeping, I started my day with some of mama's thick, buttery "stick to your ribs grits" and seized the day!

That one night at Disney was so awesome that I will forever remember all the little details; my outfit with the big stylish hoop earrings, my fluffy pink socks and teased hair, and most of all, walking around arm in arm with my friends; old and new. We were able to pack in a lifetime of memories and fun in one ten hour period. I thought of it as our one night of fantasy before the reality of adulthood took us by storm. Finals, graduation, college tours, summer jobs, orientations and so much more awaited us on the other side of Disney's gates.

It actually amazed me that I was able to stay up all night, and I always credit this event as being the turning point that set me on a totally different schedule than I had previously kept. After Grad Night I started staying up until 11 p.m. to watch the news. Afterward, I made sure I was in bed by midnight. I rose every morning at six a.m. and started my day. The way I see it, every day is another opportunity to explore and experience new things that you will not attain when you are sleeping the day away. After all, the early bird catches the worm, and for me, it all started at Disney Grad Night!

Chapter 14
Taking Notes from a Gator

Okay, so I admit it . . . I talk a lot! I'm a Chatterbox, a Chatty Cathy, the original Talkie Tessie, inquisitive, ask me anything and I will have a great answer for you, Mouth from the South! Marketing and Public Relations is my thing, and according to my Aunt Diane, who I lovingly called Aunt Di, I was born to do this. Long before Olivia Pope uttered her famous phrases, "It's handled," and "Let me do my job," I was using my gift of gab to encourage, uplift, and *spin* positivity into the lives of those surrounding me. I just didn't realize that being a compassionate, inquisitive, talkative little girl would translate into a rewarding career in the business of Marketing and Public Relations.

"Have mercy, that little girl can talk," Aunt Di told my mom one day as they ran into one another while shopping in the Oaks Mall at Macy's. "Does she always ask so many questions?"

Mom shook her head and giggled before replying. "Now, Diane, you know my baby girl is inquisitive. I'm trying to teach her that if she wants to know something, then she should ask. But you are right, that mouth can go!"

Aunt Di shook her head and let out her loud, hearty contagious laugh before saying, "Her little talking self will probably end up being a news reporter or journalist. Shoot, if she has so much to say, at least let it be for something positive!"

I was standing in the women's shoe department and heard every word they'd exchanged. To my twelve year old ears, all I heard was, "She can talk!"

For a long time, I thought my aunt disapproved of my over exuberant use of my vocal cords, but as much as I tried to stifle the urge to talk around her, I was unsuccessful. Frankly, Aunt Di was very interesting and I always found something new to talk about or inquire about when she was around. She was a graduate of the University of Florida and a Gator fan to her heart! She was everything Gator; had bumper stickers and magnets on her SUV (year round) and always had on something with the Gators on it. Heck, if I didn't want to know anything else, I wanted to know why she had so much pride for a nasty, old alligator. But that was Aunt Di, and her beloved Gators always made for good conversation.

As far back as I can remember, I hated seeing people in crisis or feeling bad, so I would always offer kind words of encouragement and advice. I often spent my free time sitting and talking to the elderly and soaking in their knowledge. They had so much wisdom and I loved being in their presence. Needless to say, my association with older people only contributed to my "talking problem." I was now equipped with the wisdom of one who was old beyond their years.

When I was 15, I started spending my summers volunteering at James Weldon Johnson middle school. Throughout the summer they hosted programs for younger children in Jacksonville, Florida. During this time, I worked with small children ages four to six. I read stories to them and held question and answer sessions to make sure they'd comprehended what I had read. I worked with them on their English and math skills, and as time went on, I even prayed for them. I found this experience rewarding and it was a perfect way for me to *communicate* with people, if you know what I mean. I now had my own audience and I loved it!

One afternoon after I had yet put poor Aunt Di through another round of Mo's mouth, she sat me down and said, "Sugar, I need to say something to you and I don't want you to take it the wrong way."

I sat and looked at Aunt Di, unblinking. In truth, I was trying to fight the urge to interrupt and tell her that Mr. Williams, the Director over the summer programs for the children, said when people start out saying, "Don't take this the wrong way," that automatically makes people take things the wrong way. But I resisted. I knew whatever she was about to say was coming from the heart, because Aunt Di was always encouraging and uplifting, and I appreciated her honesty.

"Mo, what are your plans for the future? What do you want to do when you graduate?" she asked. I was thinking about her question when she said, "I just want you to consider doing something that you love to do. And since you love to talk as much as you do, I suggest you find a job where you can talk all the time."

I looked at her again, unsure if I should consider this an insult or not. I scrunched up my nose and asked, "Aunt Di, are you trying to say that I talk too much?"

She let out the loudest laugh I had ever heard and reached out to hug me. "Baby, I've always said you could talk, but I never said you talk too much. 1 Peter 4:10 says, *'As each has received a gift, use it to serve one another, as good stewards of God's varied grace.'* That means God gives us gifts to use to help others, and, child, your gift is definitely TALKING! Use your voice to encourage and uplift."

117

From that conversation, I took my gift and I ran with it. In addition to working with the children, I used my summers to go around to different elderly members of my community just to spend time talking, gaining knowledge and letting them know that someone cared about them. There were so many of them who did not have family, and even more of them who had family that simply did not care. Well, I let them know that I cared. We would laugh, sing, clean, and, of course, TALK! It was so hard to believe these people had children, grandchildren— in some cases great grandchildren—who did not have a need for all the love and knowledge those elders possessed.

I thank my Grandmother Tiny for showing my family what being a real servant is about. She was a wonderful, committed caregiver. I often watched her care for family friends and even virtual strangers as if she shared the same bloodline with them.

Along my journey to finding Mo, I learned some important life lessons. I learned that children just want to be loved and many are not privy to the things a lot of kids take for granted. I know as a child I thought things on the outside were the same as they were on the inside of my home. I thought parents automatically loved and provided for their children. How wrong I was! I quickly gained a new understanding and respect for my parents.

I also learned to embrace those family and friends whose love and support I could *actually feel*. I learned a lot from my interactions with Aunt Di. I was an energetic, talkative child, and I'm sure there were days that I got on her nerves. Instead of using my talkativeness as a vice to criticize and condemn, she showed me how to turn it into a victory.

A lot of folks will tell you they are happy for you and they support you, but talk is cheap. I learned that not all family members want to see you succeed; sad but true. But when you have family and friends who genuinely support you and want to see you succeed, they will invest in you, even if it's something as simple as a meaningful conversation about life.

Embrace those loved ones and commit to being the best you possibly can be; not just for them, but for you. I know I have nothing but hugs and gratitude for the investment I received from Aunt Di. It's because of this that I will never stop Taking Notes from a Gator!

Chapter 15
Drive by BBQ

It was a warm day in May when I decided to visit my cousin, Renee, who lived outside of a city in Florida. We had both recently graduated from college and just needed some relaxation and girl time. When I got to her parents' house, we decided to ride over to Gainesville and visit one of her friends from The University of Florida. He was now a senior at UF and played on the football team. As we sat there chatting, we discovered that we had mutual friends, and even more remarkably, they had gotten drafted into the NFL by the San Francisco 49ers and the Tampa Bay Buccaneers. It was really exciting to know those guys had made it to the next level, and in the spirit of that excitement, Renee and I decided to continue on our road trip.

"Let's ride down to Tampa," Renee said as we walked to my car. I was driving my new candy apple red Toyota Celica with black straps and upgraded wheels. "We can ride down there and check out some of my friends and hang out a little bit," she said as we arrived at the car.

I opened my door and stood looking at Renee over the roof of the car. I was thinking that she should have known that I didn't need much convincing, since I was notorious for traveling and l loved a good road trip.

But I let her finish her spiel and then I gave her my brightest smile, a thumbs up and said, "Let's ride!" as I got into the car and buckled up my seatbelt.

We were cruising down Highway 75 South singing along with Janet Jackson. "Control, never gonna stop . . ." Renee and I sang.

We were riding with the windows rolled down enjoying the cool Florida breeze when I thought about my friend, Jocelyn, who lived in Orlando. "Hey, would you mind if we stopped in Orlando so I can see Jocelyn?" I asked Renee.

"Girl, I don't mind at all." Renee laughed. "We're not on a time schedule," she replied.

"She just started her new job at the University of Central Florida. We can surprise her at her new office," I told her as we passed by the sign for Interstate 4 that led to Orlando.

After we left Jocelyn's job, we headed toward Tampa, or so we thought; only to end up confused and helplessly lost. We drove down a random street and turned into a Dunkin Donuts where we saw several police cars parked out front.

"Is it a wonder we would find cops parked at Dunkin Donuts?" Renee mused before jumping out the car to walk over to get directions.

As we pulled away from the parking lot, we both laughed about how cliché' it was that policemen were sitting there stuffing their faces with doughnuts. So much so, that we could barely make out the directions one cop had given us.

Back on the road again, and hopefully going in the right direction, Renee and I had barely made it two blocks from the Dunkin Donuts when we started smelling barbecue. As we passed by a red brick house, we noticed cars lined up on both sides of the street. There were people in the backyard dancing and having a good time. We slowed down as we pulled up to the stop sign on the corner. A handsome young man who looked to be about our age greeted us as he walked to his car.

"Hey, pretty ladies," he said as he unlocked his car door.

"Wait, I think I know him," Renee said. "Turn around," she ordered me. "He looks like someone I went to college with."

I slowly did a U-turn and started back down the street. "Girl, I'm not thinking about that man," I said as I looked toward the house. "That barbecue smells really good. I think we should invite ourselves to the party." I laughed.

Renee stopped looking at the man who she thought she knew and stared at me with her eyebrows raised. "Oh no we won't," she replied quickly. "You're silly, Monique!" she said as she tried to read the expression on my face to see if I was serious.

I looked at Renee and laughed. "Oh come on, Renee. Don't be scared. I'll do all the talking," I said as I found a spot and parked the car across the street from the barbecue.

"Come on and stop looking so worried," I told Renee as we walked into the yard.

She was nervous and her cheeks were turning red. For the life of me I don't know how she let me talk her into crashing the barbecue, but it was too late to turn back now, because there was a slightly intoxicated man coming our way.

"Hey there," he said as he reached out to hug each of us. "Come on in," he told us as he led us into the backyard full of celebrating family members.

I looked over at Renee out the corner of my eye and I could see her staring at me with a frightened look on her face. "Just act normal," I mouthed to her as our host began to introduce us to the family.

"These are Great Uncle Irvin's girls," he said. "They came all the way from Little Rock, Arkansas," he continued on.

I snuck a peek at Renee and she looked mortified. *So I guess he wasn't just slightly intoxicated*, I thought to myself before wondering, *And who in the world is Great Uncle Irvin*? But more than that, I couldn't figure out how not one of the approximately 50 people in the yard knew who Great Uncle Irvin's kids were or what they looked like. At any rate, today Great Uncle Irvin was my daddy, Renee was my sister, and I was happy they'd never met his girls, because I was hungry and there was a barbecue rib with my name written on it!

Renee and I ate and got completely full. We had ribs, chicken, potato salad and baked beans. And our new "Cousin Raffi," the woman in charge of serving the food, even packed us plates to go as we fell into our role as long-lost cousins. We played with the kids all day long; sack races and water balloons. We had so much fun that we didn't want to leave. Surprisingly, no one ever asked us to positively identify ourselves, and that was a great thing because if they had asked, I would have had to tell the truth. But instead, they embraced us, fed us, and welcomed us with open arms. Renee and I had so much fun that we didn't end up leaving until after dark.

As we walked back to the car we marveled at how wonderful our day had gone.

"Well, so much for our trip to Tampa," I said as I unlocked the car door.

"Girl, I don't need a trip to Tampa," Renee said with a smile. "That was so much fun. I can't believe they never asked us any questions," she said as we got into the car.

"Girl, it was meant for us to enjoy this day." I laughed. "I told you to let me do the talking, but Cousin Bo did all the talking for us," I said in reference to the intoxicated man who'd introduced us as family. "So I didn't have to say a word," I said with a chuckle.

As I pulled out onto the street, I prayed this time we would be headed in the right direction, but at the same time, grateful that we had somehow ended up going in the wrong direction; landing us at this happy place. We were two adventurous cousins/sisters creating memories and feeling incredibly blessed just to be together at this moment, inhaling the aroma of hickory smoked barbecue emanating from the plates covered in foil that were sitting on the backseat; evidence of the fun day we had at our Drive by BBQ!

"I've completed all my promises to you my dear cousin S. Renee Wimberly; while you're celebrating in Heaven." Sunrise 1-23-1966 ~ Sunset 1-11-1995

Chapter 16
Bear Encounter

I was 25 years old and living in Atlanta, Georgia. I loved the hustle and bustle of city life, but being a country girl, I still craved the peaceful serenity you find out in the woods. I loved going on picnics, walking through the woods, and discovering those hidden little treasures like beautiful, clear streams and hidden shade trees where you can lay quietly and read all day. It was this that prompted me and four other friends to plan a camping trip to the North Carolina Mountains, where my friend, Yas, had previously gone camping. The trip was going to be a belated birthday celebration for all of us; as each of us had turned 25 years old over the past six months.

We were all pretty adventurous young women and had enjoyed camping before, so we enthusiastically made plans and committed ourselves to enjoying a real rustic camping experience, where we would truly relish in the great outdoors. We talked about cooking by campfire, roasting marshmallows, telling scary stories, making s'mores and sleeping in a tent. We were determined to "rough it" for the weekend; no modern amenities— just the five of us eating, drinking, exploring and getting back to nature!

We rented an SUV, packed all of our supplies and set out on our adventure on a sunny Thursday morning. We had a wonderful journey as we excitedly chatted about our jobs, relationships and the challenges we had experienced since graduating from college. The SUV was filled with non-stop chatter and good natured laughing as we covered the miles between Atlanta and North Carolina. Before we knew it, we had arrived at the campgrounds. As we got out of the vehicle, we had to stop and breathe in the beauty of our surroundings. Everything was breathtaking and the air surrounding us was crisp and clean.

"Oh my goodness, Yas," I exclaimed as I looked around. "This place is beautiful!"

The others nodded their heads in agreement.

"It seems a lot more beautiful than when I was here before," Yas said as we walked a little ways, and then simply stood admiring the beautiful mountains in the distance. We were definitely a world away from Atlanta.

"Hi, ladies," a voice called out from behind us. "I'm McClain, and this is my wife, Toddy." An animated young man who seemed to be about our age approached us with his hand held out. His wife seemed equally excited to see us as she gave us each a hug.

We introduced ourselves and learned they were newlyweds enjoying their honeymoon in the mountains. We congratulated them and left to locate a spot to make our weekend campground.

We set up our tent, dug a hole in the ground to use as a toilet, then set up lanterns for nightfall. As dusk set in, we explored the area before settling down for the evening. As night fell, we lit candles and sat around on tree stumps eating sandwiches and drinking some ice cold sweet tea, talking about life. We discussed our careers and the challenges each of us were facing working in Corporate America. As we watched a group of wild rabbits playing in the nearby trees, we mused about what directions our lives had taken and zealously made five year plans. Our first night was shaping up perfectly, and as we prepared for bed, we looked forward to the next day and discovering the hidden treasures in the North Carolina Mountains.

The next morning dawned beautifully. After breakfast, we began walking a nearby trail. It was so picturesque and lush, and with no place in particular to go, we took our time and simply explored nature. We were able to observe many wild animals in their natural habitat. Eventually we happened upon a beautiful, clear blue stream. We sat and waded our feet in the water and ate lunch, just admiring the beauty that was surrounding us.

It was dusk dark as we made our way back to the campsite. As we were walking, we saw a set of bear cubs playing alone in the forest.

"Guys, look." My friend Courtney pointed toward a glen of trees about 30 yards away.

They were three of the cutest little things I had ever seen, chasing each other and rolling around in the grass. I remember thinking that they looked just like little teddy bears. As we slowly walked by, they sensed our presence and stopped playing and began watching us.

"Hand me some bread," I told Sharie as we continued to walk.

She quickly unzipped the backpack I was wearing that held our supplies and food, then handed us each a slice of bread. We tore up the bread and tossed it to the cubs. This seemed to distract them as we used flashlights to make our way back to the campsite.

Once we made it back, we ate our dinner and talked about all the beautiful scenery and the animals we had seen along the trail; the exotic looking birds, deer, and to our dismay, we had even seen a few snakes. We laughed about the cute little bear cubs running around and I even managed to write a lot of my thoughts and experiences down in my journal before I went to sleep that night. The moon was full and I could hear all the nighttime sounds of the forest. Crickets were chirping and frogs were croaking as we laid down to rest, looking forward to our final day in the mountains.

"Mo," Brandi whispered as she shook my shoulder really hard. "Wake up," she hissed.

I opened my eyes mumbling, "What's wrong?"

"I think I just saw a bear outside," she said as her voice trembled.

I sat straight up in my sleeping bag because I thought I'd heard her say there was a bear outside of our tent. My eyes popped open as I looked around. "Oh my goodness," I screamed. "A BEAR!!! We gotta get out of here!"

My three other friends jumped up at the sound of my screams and we all began bumping into each other as we moved in five different directions. We were terrified and began to crawl around the tent, gathering up as much of our stuff as possible. Outside of my initial outburst, we made as little noise as we could until we were out of the tent.

"Grab my other shoe," Brandi whispered as she peeked outside of the tent with a flashlight.

Satisfied that our visitor was no longer there, we grabbed our backpacks and pots and pans and took off running along the trail back to our vehicle. I remembered when I was little and my grandfather told us if we ever spotted a bear that we should make as much noise as we could. So as we ran that half a mile back to the SUV, we banged and clanged those pots so loud you would've thought the circus was coming to town. We jumped in that vehicle and did not return until the next day, after spending the rest of the evening at a Marriott.

As we cautiously made our way back to the site, we admitted how scared we had been the night before and laughingly questioned whether or not Brandi had actually seen a bear. She assured us that she had and we were just happy that we had been able to get out of harm's way.

As we approached what had been our campsite, we all paused and looked at each other before looking around. Oh, Brandi had definitely seen a bear. Our tent had been ripped to shreds and all of our food was gone. Everything that we had left in our hurry to abandon camp had been tossed in a state of disarray, and it was obvious that someTHING had waited until we had gone to come back and ravage our belongings.

We gathered up what was salvageable and got the heck out of there! We hurriedly made our way back to our vehicle and only when we were safely locked inside did we stop and say a prayer of thanks. Things could have turned out a lot differently, but it hadn't. And honestly, because I believe everything happens as it is supposed to, I don't let fear stop me from doing the things I enjoy. I wasn't going to let one BIG, HUGE, GIGANTIC BEAR stop me from camping. Instead, I just made a promise to myself that on my next camping expedition, I would make sure to stay in a cabin and take MORE pots and pans; perhaps a WOK or two would ward against another Bear Encounter!

Chapter 17
A Never Forgotten Love

"What is that heavenly smell?"

The question being posed had come from the area in the main leasing office of the newly renovated apartment community where the staff would provide the residents cookies, coffee and bottled water throughout the day. The "heavenly smell" was more than likely the delicious aroma of fresh baked cookies, or perhaps it was the heady aroma of Maxwell House coffee. I didn't have time to think about it, as that voice had captured all of my attention.

I peeked furtively from behind my temporary workspace to find the face that owned that sensual voice. My attempt to be unnoticed had failed as I was looking directly into the eyes of the person I was trying to avoid . . . The one who owned "the voice."

"Good morning," I stammered as our eyes met; mine and the resident who now had my complete attention.

With an Otis Spunkmeyer cookie in hand, bottom mandible ajar, and visibly caught off guard, the owner of the voice replied, "Hi. Good morning."

It was at that moment that I discovered Love.

Love consumed my thoughts throughout that entire day. Later that evening, I welcomed the physical distraction of participating in my kickboxing fitness class. However, my drive home proved to be a challenge. I found myself daydreaming about Love, often collecting glares from passer byers as I cruised home on cloud nine. Even when I went to bed that night, I dreamed about Love. It was amazing the affect a single encounter had on me.

That very next morning I was completely preoccupied, still basking in thoughts of the day before.

"Let me get that for you."

My briefcase swung from my shoulder, Starbucks rested in hand, and my lifeline (cellphone) was glued to my ear. I hadn't noticed that Love and I had both just arrived at the main office of the apartment community. I had been going on and on to the caller on the other end of my phone about the marketing ideas that I was presenting to the property owners.

Love let me in.

"Thank you," I gestured as Love held the door for me.

Our eyes met. We became paralyzed.

Love saw me.

I quickly ended my call.

"Was the maintenance crew able to take care of your dishwasher?" I asked Love. Before parting ways at the office yesterday, I had written up a service request for the broken dishwasher Love had mentioned."

"Yes, thank you. My dishwasher is fine now," Love replied. "I'm just here to grab a cookie."

"I know; they're delicious. I try to stay away from all deliciousness. I have to start training for a marathon next fall," I said.

"Oh, are you a runner?" Love asked.

"Not really, just a fitness junkie. I'm working on becoming a certified fitness trainer."

"That sounds interesting. Maybe you can help me stay in shape." Love smiled.

"You look like you're already in pretty good shape." I eyed Love's quads. "Do you work out?"

"Yes, PT (physical training) four days a week. I'm in the US Marine Corps. I've been stationed here in Smyrna since last winter."

I smiled. "Oh, Military. I admire you guys."

Initially we were in the main leasing office. As other residents entered the building to pay their rent or turn in service requests, we moved into my office. Love grabbed a cookie on the way in.

"So how long have you worked here?" Love asked me.

"I've been on assignment here as a marketing specialist about six months. My contract is for one year."

"We should get together sometime. Maybe for lunch?"

"That sounds great!" I exclaimed. I probably said that with too much excitement.

Love bit into the cookie and winked. "You can never have too much of a good thing."

After that day, Love would come into the office just about every other day. Sometimes it was to grab a cookie or just to talk a bit. We would talk about our activities outside of work, our families or things happening in Atlanta. Then I would watch Love float out of the door. Love would often times become busy on assignment. However, I would surely get a nice voicemail or a little note sent to the office.

I eventually moved on to another assignment at another property. Still, we managed to stay in touch. Later we began to date.

As always, Love was very thoughtful and attentive. My doors were always opened for me. I was treated like royalty. Love's mother was deceased, so next to his grandmother, I became the leading lady in Love's life.

Our love grew very strong. I had never felt so esteemed and certain than when we both shared that we had known we would be a part of each other's life from the morning our eyes first met. Our relationship had all of the qualities of a love that would never end. In Love's eyes, I was a queen. We shared the best times of our lives together. We had become best friends.

As time went on, we met one another's families, went on numerous vacations together, and shared our most intimate thoughts and feelings with one another. We met each other's needs mentally, emotionally and definitely physically. Our most fascinating trips of endless intimacy were in Washington, DC and Honolulu, Hawaii. I never knew I could feel so good. Everything around me was beautiful and I felt like the most beautiful girl in the world, because that's how Love made me feel.

We made love. We moved mountains. It was never just sex. Love was gentle, sensual and affectionate. Love was compassionate. Our love was unconditional.

Life as I knew it was wonderful. I lived in a city that I adored. Atlanta was amazing and the city had proven to me that whatever I needed was available, or I had the resources to gain it. I was in a loving relationship. My professional career and my sidekick career as a fitness trainer were in full swing. I had begun training for my second marathon. I had the perfect life, or so I thought.

One night over one of our many romantic dinners, Love took my hand. "I have to ask you something."

My heart began to race. From the way he squeezed my hands, I sensed this was serious. "What is it, Babe?"

"I've been given orders to Japan in three months."

My heart sank. "Japan?" The thought of Love leaving and going to Japan made me sick to my stomach.

"I want you to join me. Will you? Come to Japan with me."

I froze. I was speechless. I released my hand from Love's grasp and sat back into my chair.

"Sweetheart, are you, okay?"

"I don't know what to say." I began thinking about my life in Atlanta. I thought about my career and my upcoming marathon. I felt fulfillment in teaching others through boot camp and kickboxing fitness classes, and helping them get into shape. I thought about my family in both Florida and Tennessee; how far I would be away from them. I wouldn't be able to jump in the car and go visit them for a weekend if I went to Japan.

"Can I have some time to think about it?" I asked.

"Sure, Sweetheart. Take all the time you need."

In the meantime, Love had business in California and scheduled a flight for me to fly out so we could drive across country together. I flew out to San Diego and Love drove us to Tampa, Florida. Love played the song "Love Shack" as we were traveling Route 66, and we sang as if we could really carry a tune. We stopped off Route 66 so I could purchase something with the Route 66 logo. I also purchased a luggage set. Too funny, but I needed it for all the traveling we would be doing.

We stopped outside of Amarillo, Texas because I wanted some fresh fruit. Love figured out very quickly that we weren't in an area of diversity. I walked into the store and greeted everyone that passed my way. Unbeknownst to me, the workers were watching me with the side eye/glare. I was clueless; I thought maybe they were admiring my cute sundress and sandals. I remember asking the guy stocking the canned goods to help me find the Lorna Doone shortbread cookies and a bag of butter popcorn. He looked at me as if he had seen a ghost.

I had no idea the fact that I was African American was the cause of their actions. But Love did. Love walked over to me and said, "Get what you want and meet me at the register." Love's voice was soft and always sweet to me regardless of the situation. But I could sense the urgency, so I did just as he'd asked.

The manager walked over, bagged the items I had placed on the belt, handed me the bag and said, "Have a nice day." He stared at me with a raised brow for a couple seconds before I finally got the hint.

Love had given me the money to pay, but they wanted us out of their store quickly. Didn't have to tell me twice. I said, "Thank you," and left.

We ended up staying overnight in Albuquerque, New Mexico and had a delightful evening. We ate some really good Mexican food and watched a movie on HBO in our hotel room. We fell asleep to the most peaceful night breeze. The weather there was just serene.

We enjoyed this time to reflect on relaxation and all the adoring time we had spent together. Did I mention that from San Diego to Tampa, Florida, I only drove a total of two hours? I know; Love didn't mind driving me cross-country and asked that I just nap and sight see. How sweet was that?

We made it safely to Tampa. Love was able to see family and friends before leaving for deployment. Love left for Japan and gave me more time than reasonable to decide if I would be following behind. As the days, weeks and months went by, I felt pressure. I began to avoid the question all together. Our long distance relationship continued and Love began making arrangements for me to come to Japan . . . Since I hadn't actually declined the offer.

Since I hadn't declined, a part of me felt sure that I would just go ahead and move to Japan. The closer it got to the time I was scheduled to leave, cold feet set in. I felt really torn. Would I take a risk and trust having love, or would I stay in my comfort zone?

One morning I awoke and called Love.

"I can't," I said into the phone receiver.

"You can't what, Sweetheart?"

"I can't. I can't come to Japan."

"What do you mean? The movers are going to be there to pack your things for you in just a few days. Please think about this," Love pleaded with me.

"I'm sorry," I cried. "I just can't."

My decision not to join Love in Japan took a major toll on our relationship. We loved each other dearly, yet began to drift apart. The distance was too great. We often talked about how we felt about my decision. The pain and hurt was obvious. The telephone calls became few and far between.

Love moved to D.C. a couple years or so later after being assigned back to the States. We began to communicate more frequently, often discussing the past. We both knew that we would not be able to overcome the bridge that Japan had put between us. We agreed that we'd experienced a never forgotten love that would always be registered in our hearts. We knew that this was one love that we may never experience again in this lifetime.

I moved on without Love, often playing our relationship back in my head. I missed out and felt regret for years thereafter. I had no one to blame but myself for letting Love get away. This affected me in such a way that I vowed that I would never let the next real love get away. I'd follow real love to the moon if need be.

Chapter 18
The Peachtree Road Race

Atlanta's Peachtree Road Race is the largest 10K in the world, and for eight years straight, I was one of the estimated 60,000 participants. The event is sponsored by the Atlanta Track Club. For 46 years running, it has been held on the Fourth of July weekend and has become a time honored tradition. As it was becoming a tradition in the city of Atlanta, it was also becoming a tradition amongst me and my friends. A small group of us began flying from our homes in various parts of the country to Atlanta every year for a sort of "Friends Reunion." The first year we had such a blast we decided to make it a yearly gathering.

The night before the race, we would hang out and meet as many new people as possible. We would introduce ourselves and share a few laughs and camaraderie with others who were there for the race as well. For five out of the eight years, we all stayed separately with friends and family who resided in the area, but for the other three years we stayed at a hotel in Buckhead and really let the good times roll!

We would reserve one hotel room and all eleven of us would stay up late laughing, playing cards and catching up on what was going on in each other's lives. After all, we only got together once a year, so believe me when I say there was a lot of catching up to do.

The morning of the race always dawned beautifully. We would be at the start line at five a.m. with cups of coffee and bananas or a bagel. Between the eleven of us, it seemed like we knew everyone at the starting line. If we hadn't met them the night before, it seemed like we knew them from previous years. And if by chance we didn't know them when we arrived, by the time the gun went off, we had certainly made their acquaintance; this included the volunteers as well as the police officers on duty. In fact, we have a very special officer who has become our friend over the years. Her name is Officer Kim Jones and she always looks out for us. The Peachtree Road Race would not be the same without her presence.

Along the course of the race, there are thousands of spectators. We have been fortunate to have quite a few friends who aren't runners to stand along the route with ice cold water, frozen grapes, and pretzels to keep our energy and motivation up, because that 6.2 mile course is not easy. But it is FUN, and I will tell the truth, it usually takes my crew a while longer to complete the race because we are so busy being sociable; laughing, hugging and chatting with all the spectators along the way. It's not easy being a social butterfly, but hey, somebody's got to do it.

I've had so many memorable races, and one year the finish was a bit more memorable than normal. That particular race started out just as the others. As I was known to do, I parked my car a few miles away from the finish line so I could walk to the start and get my warm up in. On this morning, I was so excited that I accidentally locked my keys, money and cell phone in the car, but I was determined not to let that mishap stop my progress. I ran the entire race, and afterward, I stood around eating popsicles and socialized with my friends as if all was right in my world.

As many of them readied themselves to leave and began making their way to the Marta train, I began the trek back to my car. No one asked if I was okay to walk back alone, and I never mentioned having locked my keys and personal effects in the car, so no one knew my plight. I was exhausted and my legs were so tired, but I dug in and ran a few miles and walked the rest of the way back to my car. I ended up going into the Embassy Suites and calling my cousin, who had an extra key to my car, to come to my rescue.

I ended up waiting for another hour or so because he was shopping at the Mall of Georgia, but I didn't complain. I had done what I set out to do, and therefore, I was okay with that little speed bump. While I waited alone in the hotel for my cousin, I was a little bit sad and thoroughly exhausted, but God saw me through, and hallelujah, I had successfully completed another Peachtree Road Race!

Over the years I became an avid runner; having participated in many races. But I can honestly say the Peachtree Road Race is one of my favorites, because it is one of the most heartwarming and unforgettable races I've ever participated in. Like many events similar to this one, there's always that one moment when you thank God for being there because you have the opportunity to make a difference in someone's life. My moment came one race morning when I parked my car several miles away from the finish line, as was my habit. As always, my intent was to use the distance to warm up for the race and get focused.

As I was passing a group of kids sitting on the curb at Peachtree near Piedmont Road, I had the blessing of hearing a little boy tell the kid next to him, "This is my first time coming to the Peachtree Road Race and it looks like a lot of fun. I'm really excited to see all of these famous runners and walkers. I know some of them will have to walk up the hill near Piedmont Hospital."

I smiled over at them as I continued to walk because I knew exactly what hill he was talking about. It was a hill that could be quite challenging to some. Once I got past them I heard the little boy's final words, and my heart shattered into a thousand pieces.

"If I had legs, I would run the Peachtree Road Race," he said.

I so wanted to turn around and say something motivational and uplifting, but for the first time, I was speechless.

After the race I told my friends all about the little boy and his desire to run. Just as I was heartbroken, so were my friends. I had spent the entire race thinking about how often we able bodied folks take our limbs for granted. After talking to my friends, we decided that we wanted to do something to put a smile on his face and somehow make his first Peachtree Road Race even more special for him. But what could we do?

My friends and I talked about how blessed we were to have the use of our limbs. We all came together for a moment just to say, "Thank you, Lord," and ask God for direction, because we realized that we were standing in one of those moments where beautiful memories were made.

As I stood drinking a bottle of water, I thought about the pride I felt each time I received my Road Race t-shirt. Let's face it; many people participate year after year just to be able to say, "I survived the Peachtree Road Race." They can't wait to participate in the revered tradition of putting on the finisher's t-shirt. That part of the race is almost as big as the Road Race tradition itself, and so it was decided; I would find the little boy and give him my t-shirt. By the time we located him, my friends had also decided to donate their shirts to his friends.

His eyes lit up like Christmas morning, and so I knew that it was meant for me to park my car almost six miles away from the finish line. And it was meant for me to give up my treasured t-shirt, because on that day it meant so much more to a child who was unable to walk, much less run. It was just a status symbol for me, but for him, it was a lasting memory of the day he got to participate in the Peachtree Road Race t-shirt tradition.

Afterward, we lined Peachtree Road near Lenox Mall, set up our chairs and card tables, and waited for the fireworks . . . The perfect ending to yet another successful Peachtree Road Race.

Chapter 19
Short Lived

"Important encounters are planned by the souls long before the bodies see each other." ~Paulo Coelho

My soul connected with Champ's in the produce section of Harry' Farmer's Market in Duluth, Georgia on a sweltering Wednesday afternoon in June. According to my old college friends, if one was seeking companionship, Harry's was the place to be on Wednesday evenings between the hours of four and seven. I remember laughing at my friend Sondra as she tried to explain the allure of Harry's.

"I'm serious, girl; you can meet just about anyone at Harry's," Sondra said. "That little market is jumping between four and seven. It's like happy hour in there!"

At the time I thought that was the funniest thing I had ever heard. Who goes to the supermarket to meet a mate? I mean, who is really desperate enough to troll the aisles of a market in an effort to find a date? I shook my head in wonder, but on the inside a little voice said, "You are." I had to admit, though, I was indeed intrigued.

"Those look pretty good," a voice said from behind me, immediately giving me a warm, peaceful feeling all over.

I dropped the golden delicious apple I was holding and hesitantly turned around to look into the warmest set of dark brown eyes I had ever seen. "I was thinking the same thing," I managed to get out. "I guess I'll try a few of them. I hear this is the freshest produce in Atlanta."

Champ laughed and said, "Well, I don't know about that part, but I'm here because I heard this is the best place to meet beautiful ladies."

"Between four and seven, huh?" I smirked.

Champ shrugged with a sheepish grin, arms spread wide, and we both began to laugh. Champ had an unforgettable, hearty laugh that seemed to resonate directly from the soul. At the time I remember thinking, *I could listen to this laugh for a lifetime.*

Champ and I became inseparable from that day forth, and we both recognized immediately that we were supposed to be together. We forged a bond that was like no other, instantly becoming an integral part of each other's lives; sharing a love for family, friends, and a rich appreciation for the life and the love we were blessed with. We appreciated every moment we had to spend together, because we knew that time was not promised. You see, my Champ was a proud member of the United States Army, and at any given time, duty might call and Champ would have to answer. Therefore, we did everything together and connected on a heightened spiritual and emotional level in such a short period of time, that we could only conclude that we were indeed soulmates.

Champ had such a loving spirit that I found myself pouring out my soul during our lengthy conversations. It felt like we had known each other our entire lives. Champ was caring and supportive and never above compromise. Feeling warm, safe and protected made my heart melt. I can only guess being the youngest child of eight protective siblings produced a person who felt loved, supported and self-assured.

In our relationship, there was no pretense. We were comfortable being ourselves, so we didn't experience a lot of the small things that some couples go through when one or both of them are insecure. We made each other better and made no bones about telling each other just how blessed we were to have both been in the produce aisle of Harry's on that particular Wednesday.

As we fell in love, we fell into a comfortable routine of sharing each other's space. We made sure to always make time for each other and planned our time together meticulously. We had date night once a week and shared lunch once a week as well. Once a month we would pull out the after five wear and enjoy dinner at a nice, expensive restaurant. I loved dressing up for those monthly dates. We planned picnics in the park and spent a lot of time just being together. Three mornings a week, without fail, we would meet at the gym at 5:00 a.m., and afterward we took turns cooking breakfast since we only lived a mile apart. We would go bowling, mountain biking, skiing in Colorado, attend high school sporting events and plays. One thing we absolutely loved to do was go to Sam's Club and sample all the free food and snacks they would have available while shopping for groceries, since Harry's Farmers Market was now off limits. We always managed to come out of there with our hearts full of laughter and stomach's full of junk food.

One of the biggest things we had in common was our mutual love for travel. We both enjoyed exploring different places and seeing the world, which was the subject of our one and only argument.

"I think we should drive to Naples Beaches in Florida. That way we can see more sights along the way," Champ told me one night as we discussed our trip.

This did not sit well with me because I was a world traveler and I loved flying from one destination to another. I always thought we could save more time by flying, and that way we would have more time to explore.

"Well, I want to fly," I said with finality. "I love flying among the clouds, and anyway, it saves time. It's just practical," I said as an afterthought.

Champ looked at me and said, "Everywhere I go with the military I have to fly. I would rather just load up the car, take our time, explore as many places as we can and relax. Forget practicality!"

Needless to say, we laughed about this silly argument as we DROVE cross-country from Los Angeles to Naples, Florida. One thing I learned from my relationship with Champ was to always let love win.

While we traveled, we often marveled at how remarkable it was that we shared so many common traits. The traits we did not share somehow provided a balance for us. For example, I hated shopping.

Growing up, my mom always shopped for me. Thankfully my love didn't have a problem with shopping, and took up where my mom left off. Champ agreed to always be my personal shopper and even surprised me during our trip by stopping at the mall and purchasing me a diamond necklace and earrings that literally took my breath away. I felt so special receiving this beautiful gift, but Champ made me feel even more special by saying, "I would give you my last because you appreciate who I am and I feel the presence of your love—even when you're away."

As we drove, we would talk for hours on end about our lives and our hopes for the future. We shared our most memorable moments from our long weekend cruise to the Bahamas and our "mental escape trip" to Boca Raton, Florida. We captured as many moments as possible, taking nothing for granted. We loved loving one another and being in love. Champ loved serving in the military and was very proud to be in service to our country, but we agreed when the next deployment was over, we would make a formal commitment and become engaged. The intense love and mutual respect we shared was something we both needed and both agreed we DESERVED.

Champ had the ability to know how I was feeling before I could verbalize it. We were very in tune with each other and never missed an opportunity to say, "I love and appreciate you."

I was in awe of this new, intense love that I had been blessed with. Right up until this very moment, I can say without reservation, in my Champ, I found everything I ever wanted and needed.

For ten days we drove without a care in the world. We took our time taking in the scenery and the amazing beauty of nature; making an unplanned detour to see the Grand Canyon, and even taking the time to stop at each state line to take pictures. Every day we fell more and more in love and bonded in a way that astounded us both.

I remember telling Champ, "We have a life filled with love that most people never experience." And it was true.

Champ would often tell me, "Monique, darling, you are the platinum of my life and I treasure the life we share."

We never took our love for granted. We lived each day in truth and love; promising to always speak to one another from the heart and not from the head. We practiced our love and we never forgot to give thanks to God for bringing us together.

After our first year together, we spent our Sundays worshipping together at both of our church services. Early morning service was spent at my church, Saint Philip A.M.E. in Atlanta, Georgia, and then we would attend morning service at Champ's church, Victory World Church in Norcross, Georgia. We didn't consider it a sacrifice, but more so a great opportunity for spiritual growth together. Afterward, of course, we would discuss the services over brunch; always challenging each other to reach new heights of spiritual and self-awareness.

I loved the lazy afternoons when I could look across the table and see my love, admiration, and growth reflecting in the eyes of another. It transcended me to higher heights.

They say soulmates come into your life to awaken the different parts of you in order for your soul to reach a higher level of consciousness, but sadly, once this occurs, there is usually a physical separation. Champ was lost to me on a bitter winter morning in the line of duty while serving in Afghanistan. My Champion is now resting peacefully amongst other heroes in Arlington National Cemetery in Arlington, Virginia. As for me, I am just grateful to have known a love so great, and to this day, I carry Champ in my heart. I enjoy each day, take nothing for granted, and embrace each beautiful moment I am able

to share with family and friends. Through the love of my life, I learned

that life is a beautiful gift, but it is often Short Lived...

Chapter 20
The Game Changer

The year was 2002; spring was the season and March Madness was in full swing. My older sister, Lisa—my beautiful, brilliant, and loving shero—was bravely fighting a losing battle with liver disease, and my heart was breaking. From the time I was a little girl, I looked up to my sister. Not only was she very pretty, but she was kind. She had such a gentle spirit that I don't think she made one enemy in her lifetime. Lisa was the type of person who painstakingly built all of her relationships with love and honesty. Not only did I love her, I actually liked her as a person and loved being able to tell people she was MY big sister.

Even though we were four years apart, Lisa and I shared a love for sports. We would spend all of our free time discussing basketball and football. If we weren't talking about sports, we were watching them on television or in person. Lisa and her best friend, Veronica Johnson, would often let me tag along with them to basketball or football games. Roni, as Veronica was affectionately known, was much like Lisa; she had a lot of associates who wanted to become friends. Veronica and Lisa somehow developed a comfortable sisterhood that was so honest and true, that Lisa made Veronica promise if anything ever happened to her, that Veronica would take care of me; become a surrogate big sister.

Every year in March, Lisa and I would get into these intense discussions on which college teams would make it to the "Sweet Dance" and the NCAA Men's Final Four. During the tournaments we would challenge each other on which teams would advance in the college brackets. For years we looked forward to our March Madness traditions because we had so much fun teasing and debating with each other . . . Until it all came to an abrupt halt in the spring of 2002.

As greatly as we wanted to, we couldn't do much debating because Lisa was not feeling well. I remember going to see her in Jacksonville and arriving to her house late at night. As I dozed in the chair beside Lisa's bed, I was awakened by her soft voice.

"Mo, I have three wishes for my life," she whispered.

I sat up in the chair and shook my head quickly to ward off sleep. "Three wishes," I repeated groggily. "What are they?" I asked quietly.

Lisa smiled warmly as her eyes welled up with tears. "I trust that God allows me to see my fortieth birthday," she said while holding up one finger. Her birthday was three and a half weeks away. "I trust that my son will get a scholarship to college." She raised two fingers. Her son had been waiting to hear back from the college of his choice regarding his scholarship application. "And finally, I trust that you, my little sister, will be the one to find my first strand of gray hair." Lisa laughed as she held up three fingers and stared at me with a resigned look in her eyes.

My heart felt like it would break into a thousand pieces because it was at that moment I realized my sister was facing her own mortality, but I wasn't ready to face the possibility. I hugged Lisa tightly and told her, "God's got you, Sis, and we've got each other."

A few weeks later I received a call from Mom. I remember it was the first week in April and I was at work. "Lisa is in the hospital in Gainesville," Mom said solemnly.

Immediately, I informed Gigi, my supervisor, and I got into my car and left work. I didn't go home to pack a bag or call anyone to let them know what was going on. I just got into my car and began the long drive from Buford, Georgia to Gainesville, Florida. In hindsight, I don't know how I made it because I was driving on autopilot. I was alone in my car; alone with my thoughts, and that was not a good place to be. My mind was stayed on Lisa. How was I going to go on without my big sister? Who was going to encourage me to fulfill my dreams, and who was going to debate me about college basketball? I didn't want my nephew to have to grow up without his mother, and I was worried about the impact Lisa's illness was having on my mom.

I arrived in Gainesville around two a.m. and planned to see Lisa first thing in the morning, but that was not to be. The doctor called Mom and told her they were transporting Lisa by air to Hospice of Jacksonville. I was confused. I didn't know why they were transporting her, but I made myself believe they wanted her to be near family so she could reap the benefits of the family's tender loving care.

I honestly did not know what Hospice Care was about, but I could look at my mom and see that she was numb. Her eyes held a sadness that I had never seen before, and I felt completely helpless. I needed someone to explain Hospice Care to me and I needed Mom to smile and tell me that everything was going to be okay; that Lisa was going to be okay. But again, that was not to be.

I watched my mom stare out the car window as we made the 45 minute ride to Jacksonville. I wanted to say something that would take her pain away, but I couldn't find the words. All I could do was stand by helpless as my sister lay unconscious and my mother sat heartbroken.

"Aunt Di," I cried into the phone. "I'm here at the hospital with Mom. Lisa is sick and I don't know what to do. Mom isn't talking and I don't know what to say to make her feel better." Tears were rolling down my face as I listened to Aunt Di's soothing voice. I don't remember what she said to me on that day, all I know was her tone was comforting and I drew strength from across the miles.

We had been at Hospice a few minutes and a doctor came out to speak with us. I was listening to him explain what was to be their role in Lisa's transition, and I sat quietly listening to every heartbreaking word, determined to be strong for Lisa and my mom.

"May I see my sister?" I asked the doctor afterward.

"Yes you can," he replied. "We've given her some morphine to help ease her discomfort as she transitions," he said, "but you may sit with her."

I walked into the room and the only thing I could think about was Lisa's three wishes. I kept hearing her voice over and over again telling me she trusted that she would make it to her fortieth birthday on April 7th, her son would get a college scholarship, and I would find her first strand of gray hair. My head began to spin and my breathing accelerated. I ran out of the room and made it to the restroom right before my body was wracked by a severe panic attack.

A few hours later, two doctors came to speak with us to explain the dying process to our family. Lisa was settled in resting peacefully. I went into her room and noticed that someone had brushed her long hair back neatly and put it into a ponytail. As I walked around her bed, I rubbed Lisa's beautiful face. As I brushed back a few stray hairs, I noticed one long, shiny gray hair.

"Mom, look," I whispered excitedly. I motioned for all of my relatives to come and look at Lisa's gray strand. When I got a few peculiar stares, I realized that I was the only one who knew about Lisa's three wishes.

As we sat around her room, my nephew walked in. He walked up to his mother's bed and kissed her gently on the forehead. My heart broke for him because I knew it would be hard going on without his mother. He looked over at me and Mom and smiled sadly before taking a deep breath.

"I will be headed to college in the fall," he said proudly. "I'm going to FAMU on a scholarship!" He'd received the news.

My breath caught in my throat and tears came to my eyes as I realized that two of Lisa's wishes had been fulfilled. I looked over at my sister and said a silent prayer for her. Tomorrow was to be her birthday, but tomorrow was not promised to her.

I chose to believe Lisa would live to see her birthday, and so I planned a surprise birthday celebration for her. I called Publix and ordered a cake and invited our relatives to come and celebrate with us. Lisa's born day emerged beautifully; everything was gloriously green and butterflies fluttered outside of her window. I remember looking out at the brilliant sunlight and thanking God for sparing my sister's life and fulfilling her last wishes. We picked up the cake, and for a moment, I just stared down at the words on it that read: *"Happy Birthday, Lisa. We Love You!"*

Happy Birthday to you. Happy Birthday to you. Happy Birthday, Dear Lisa. Happy Birthday to Youuuu. How old are you? How old are you? How old are you? How old are you? She's 40 years old. She's 40 years old. She's 40 years old. SHE'S 40 YEARS OLD!!!

We softly sang the birthday song to Lisa and I remember thinking I had never heard anything so beautiful. Lisa, my beautiful, brilliant, loving big sister had lived to see her fortieth birthday; thus fulfilling her three wishes. I remember looking down at Lisa's pretty face and thinking that she must have been pleased, because she had the most peaceful smile on her face. Although I was grief stricken, I was happy and proud once again to tell the world that she was MY big sister.

I had to leave later on that night because I had a mandatory inspection at work the next morning. I didn't hit the road until after eight p.m., and I knew I had a long trip back to Atlanta. As soon as I got into the car, I began to cry. I cried and I cried until I was all cried out. By that time my eyes were severely swollen. I could barely see out of them and decided to exit the interstate and grab a cup of coffee. I sat in my car in the Waffle House parking lot for a few minutes, trying to get myself together before I walked in and ordered a coffee.

My waitress looked at me with concern; asking if I was all right. I told her I was and then walked to the restroom to check my appearance. I looked ghastly. My eyes looked like I had been on the losing end of a heavyweight boxing match. I vaguely remember seeing a bunch of bikers as I exited the restroom. I grabbed my coffee and walked to my car. Once I made it to my car, I sat behind the wheel and a dam broke inside of me. My heart began aching as I poured out all of my grief. I banged on the steering wheel as I cried out Lisa's name and prayed. I rested my head on the steering wheel as my tears began to dissipate, but then reality set in that I could barely see, and I had to get back to Atlanta by morning.

I heard a rapping on the driver's side window.

I looked up to see the waitress. "Are you okay, Sweetie?" she asked through the window. I looked behind her and saw a bunch of bikers clad in leather vests and jeans. I was too distraught to worry about whether or not I was in harm's way. I rolled down the window a little bit and the waitress asked again if I was okay.

"My sister is in hospice in Jacksonville and I have to get back to Atlanta for an inspection at work," I cried while shaking my head hopelessly.

One of the bikers came to my window and replied, "Listen, young lady. I have a daughter and I would want someone to help her if she was having difficulty getting home." The other bikers nodded their assent in the background. "Where do you live in Atlanta?" he asked.

I answered that I lived off the Mall of Georgia Exit. One of the other bikers acknowledged that he knew where that exit was, and then shortly thereafter, we were on our way.

For over three hours I was surrounded by a dozen bikers on Harley Davidson motorcycles. They surrounded my car as I drove back to Atlanta; until I put my right turn signal on at Exit 115 off 85 North in Buford, Georgia. Once I exited they did a U-turn and blew their horns at me. I drove into Preston Hills at Mill Creek Apartments at seven a.m. on Monday morning. I ran inside to quickly prepare for work and had just sat on the side of my bed when the telephone on my nightstand rang. My heartbeat accelerated because deep in my heart I already knew . . .

"She just left us," Mom's sad voice said on the other end.

My sister, Lisa, transitioned on April 8, 2002 and we celebrated her Home Going Service on April 13 with heavy hearts.

Every year since then, I honor Lisa's love for college basketball by watching March Madness and attending the NCAA Women's Final Four. It was our mutual love for college basketball that bonded us and gave me a way to celebrate Lisa in a manner that I know is pleasing to her. Before her passing, I loved the moments Lisa and I spent together, but her death became a game changer for me. Now, March Madness is not just about the game of basketball. It's a reminder of the special bond I shared with my brilliant, beautiful and kind big sister, Lisa. And it's a reminder to always celebrate life today, for it's not promised to us tomorrow.

Chapter 21
Doubt, Fear and Unbelief

One afternoon, as I made my way through the parking lot of Northlake Mall, I distractedly looked for a place to park my car that was not too far away from my part-time waitressing job at Ruby Tuesday. On that particular day, for some strange reason I was not myself. Lately, I had been thinking about something my Aunt Di had said to me as a teenager. I kept hearing her voice over and over telling me, "You should consider getting a job where you can talk all the time."

As I walked into the restaurant, I greeted the hostess and other waitresses with a warm greeting and a big smile. No matter how distracted I was, I still made sure I practiced good manners and greeted everyone when I walked into a room, as my parents had taught me.

"Thank you, please come and see us again real soon," I told my customers as they left my section. As I started clearing the table, I picked up my tip, a ten dollar bill, and noticed that there was a note written on the receipt. I mumbled the note to myself. "Great service, Monique. You are an incredibly friendly and witty waitress. I enjoyed hearing you talk!"

I smiled at the compliment but I noticed that the note hadn't read, "I enjoyed talking to you," but instead had read, "I enjoyed hearing you talk."

Oh my goodness! Had I talked too much? Once again, Aunt Di's words echoed inside my head. *"You should consider getting a job where you can talk all the time."* I had to admit that I loved talking to people and helping them through their problems. And then I knew—at that very moment standing in Ruby Tuesday on a Thursday night—that I wanted to be a motivational speaker.

I was one month out of undergrad school, and aside from talking to the children at the summer program at James Weldon Johnson in Jacksonville, Florida, I had never stood in front of a crowd to speak. In fact, at JWJ, I didn't stand in front of a real crowd; I had only read to a classroom of children. Motivational speaking was different, though. There would be no books to read and I would have to come up with my own topics. I would have to be entertaining and funny, and most of all, I would have to be able to provide motivation.

"Can I do that?" I asked myself over and over again. While I got nervous just thinking about it, the need and desire to do something meaningful was stronger than any fear I experienced.

The next night I decided to sit down and come up with a plan of action. I had just made it home from work, and though I was tired, I wanted to at least start the process. I turned on the television and turned the volume down low so I could think clearly. I grabbed my journal out of my purse and sat down on the couch. On the top of the first free page I wrote the words: "Motivational Speaking." Underneath that I made two columns. The first column was reserved for Pros. I began writing: *Source of income, *travel, *meeting new people. Next I began writing the cons: *NO EXPERIENCE (in all capital letters). As I was pondering other cons to write down, I glanced up at the TV screen. The television was tuned in to Fox 5 News Atlanta, and there was a Fulton County Principal discussing an upcoming Career Day event. I went and stood in front of the screen and increased the volume. They were looking for volunteers.

"Oh my goodness," I said out loud. The timing couldn't have been more perfect. I wrote down the number that was scrolling across the bottom of the screen and made plans to call the school and volunteer my services to speak at Career Day. I was excited, but there was also a nervous tingle in the pit of my stomach at the thought of speaking in front of a crowd. Regardless of my doubt, I was going to do it.

173

I called the number on the following Monday and was told there were two available slots for speakers; one at a high school and one at an elementary school. I quickly chose the elementary school because the last thing I needed on my first experience was a bunch of rambunctious teenagers challenging me. Oh no, that would have been a disaster. I preferred to ease in one foot at a time with the youngsters. Surely they wouldn't realize I was a newbie.

"Good Morning," I started out. "My name is Monique Chandler and today I am going to teach you how to get what you want from your parents every time you ask," I said as my voice caught in my throat. I looked into the faces of those fourth graders and my nervousness increased, but I continued on despite the sweat that had broken out on my upper brow.

Clearing my throat, I continued on. "One way to win your mother over is to stop and pick a flower on your way home from school. When your mom comes in from work, meet her at the door and say, 'I love you, Mom.'"

A few of the children laughed as I struggled on.

"When your dad is outside cutting the grass, go into the yard and take him a nice, cold glass of fresh lemonade and say, 'Thank you, Daddy, for keeping our yard clean.' He will appreciate the effort from you," I finished relieved. I wanted to end my presentation with a Q & A session, so I asked the students if anyone had any questions.

The first hand to go up was a young kid whose name, according to his nametag, was Jason.

"Yes, Jason?" I asked. "What is your question?"

Jason stood up and swiped the long blond hair out of his eyes and stared at me with confusion on his face. "Ma'am, why are you so nervous talking to us? We're just little kids," he said and sat down.

There was a murmur of agreement throughout the room. I looked around and realized that Jason was right. They *were* just little kids, and as much as I loved talking to children and mentoring them, how was it feasible that I was nervous in front of them? In fact, as much as I loved talking to people, and seemingly they enjoyed listening to me talk, why would I let my fears keep me from doing what I loved to do?! I was born to talk and I was determined that is what I would do.

From that day forward, I went on to speak at hundreds of events; some of them small and others with groups up to 2,500 people. I can honestly say that I left my doubt, fear, and unbelief back in that fourth grade classroom.

I have been fortunate over the years to add many layers to my presentations. I must say some of them are hilariously funny and motivating, with titles like "Feeling Better" and "My Gas is Gone." I would say we all have gas from time to time; release it and move forward. So I say to you that if there is something in life you long to do, release any doubt, fear and unbelief and do it!

Chapter 22
Life Changes

"Love is patient and kind; love does not envy or boast; it is not arrogant or rude. It does not insist on its own way; it is not irritable or resentful; it does not rejoice at wrongdoing, but rejoices with the truth. Love bears all things, believes all things, hopes all things, endures all things."

As I stood looking in the mirror, the words from 1 Corinthians 13:4-7 kept playing over and over in my head. I continued to comb my hair while trying to suppress the words that had once been so beautiful to me, but now were serving as a constant reminder of what was missing in my marriage.

I put down the hair comb and stood face to face with my reflection. "You did things the right way. You gave it your all," I said to myself. "He tried to break you, but he did not succeed, and you deserve peace," I finished before picking up my comb. As much as I wanted my marriage to work, I had admitted a long time ago that we were in the marriage for two separate reasons, and it was finally time to have my day in court.

When we married I had certain expectations. I expected us to love one another. I expected us to provide companionship. I expected friendship and I expected laughter. As hard as it was to fathom, our foundation was never solid because these things were by no means reciprocated. In hindsight, I could see my marriage was destined to fail because it was not built on the basis of *mutual* trust, respect, fidelity and love. So it was just a matter of time before our weak foundation began to crumble. It was inevitable that we would experience the life changes that many couples go through.

My journey through this experience taught me so many things about life and even more valuable things about me; like I'm worthy and I'm able. And even though my union failed, that did not mean I had failed. Through my life changes I learned that, YES, I deserved to be happy, and my happily ever after was not tied to another person or even a fairytale marriage. It did not depend on anyone else but me!

From the very beginning we seemed to have separate agendas. I thought we had married for better or for worse, but he was on a different sheet of music. He constantly found new ways of deception, and by the time I figured out one game, he was on to the next. I became so adept at investigating, that the P.I. Company I sought to hire wanted to hire me instead. I was living a miserable existence and I felt lost. I was one that would show up and be present and asleep at the same time. I had reached that point.

I clearly remember the days when I would get off work and intentionally drive I-285 from Dunwoody around back to I-85 North because I knew I would get stuck in traffic for hours. That would delay my arrival at home. I was very stressed and unhappy and my marital home was not a peaceful, safe haven for me. From time to time I would sleep in my car parked inside the garage because it was more peaceful. I knew this was not how love was supposed to be, but like so many, I didn't like the thought of life changes, but the blatant disrespect was pushing me away further and further by the day.

The writing was on the wall. Everything he did was right there staring me in the face. It truly baffled me how a person could be so boldly transparent in their wrongdoings, but he just didn't care. For a long time I worried about what others would say, but I knew in my heart that despite what the world would think, I had to navigate my way back to me. Walking away from a life of wealth and affluence was something that a lot of people have difficulty wrapping their minds around, but believe me, when it comes down to having your peace of mind versus having material worth, there's really no comparison. Sitting alone in a house full of beautiful things while you put all your effort into pretending that you don't see the obvious signs of infidelity can wreak havoc on your self-esteem, emotional stability, and even the strongest person can experience moments of self-doubt.

After several years of isolating from others the fact that I was unhappily married, I sat down with my God sister first, then with two dear friends on separate occasions. I shared with them what I had been dealing with. They allowed me to talk and not once did any of them pass judgment on me. Talking to them really helped me to focus, and I became determined to come up with an exit strategy. I knew in doing this there would be some people who did not agree with my decisions and that I would surely lose a few folks along the way.

Sometimes when you lose a spouse, you lose the family you married into as well. Sadly, the children I supported became distant and walked away. Married friends with whom we socialized disappeared as if they had never been there. The ones who didn't change or disappear were the same ones who always supported me from the beginning; my parents.

My father told me, "Some parents would be angry, some would be disappointed and some parents would be upset about their daughter having put up with so much alone, and the fact that it ended in life changes. But we love you dearly and you always have a place to call home."

They supported me through the ups and the downs of my marriage even though, unbeknownst to me, they never liked the dynamics of my relationship. But they respected me enough to let me make my own decisions and just kept their distance until I needed them. And like they always did, in the end they supported me and loved me through the pain.

At the end of the marriage, I celebrated! I stood in front of a judge and told him, "Your honor, all I want is my name and my integrity." It did not matter that I was walking away from a wealth of material things and money. I knew that I could acquire those things again through hard work. No amount of money or possessions was worth the peace of mind I gained on that day. I threw myself a "Thank God for Life Changes" celebration and committed to moving on. There were certain things I had to make peace with and certain lessons I had to learn before I reached that happy place.

I had to learn that it was okay to take my time getting back to me. I had to go through what I had to go through; I couldn't look at anyone else's situation and judge how much time was sufficient to mourn my marriage. My going through was MY going through, and in order for me to reach a place of peace, I had to experience a wide range of emotions. Even though I was happy, at the same time, it still felt like a death had occurred. I was frightened to embark on a new life, but I was also filled with anticipation for the new and great changes that were going to occur. Change is a scary thing, and even when it is a good change, it still involves uprooting and starting over again. We have to be very careful about changing so many things at once. Quitting cold turkey is not for everyone, and doing so much at one time can be overwhelming to some.

I learned the importance of taking time for myself. I spent a great deal of time by myself just learning to love me. I took mini weekend vacations as often as I could because I had to learn how to make me and my happiness a priority; no one is going to take care of my heart like I can. I treated myself to the spa once a quarter for a "day of beauty." I even spent a few days alone at the Chateau Elan Winery & Resort in the North Georgia foothills in Braselton to journal and mentally take a break. I treated myself and loved on myself as often as I could. I took a four day weekend and spent it in the luxury of the Ritz Carlton. I even ordered a bath butler to draw my bath. I spoiled myself simply because I deserved it. I learned to understand that life changes can happen to anyone, and like most life lessons, it involves growth and maturity. What is also important is that we *own* our mistakes and learn from them. It's pointless to keep making the same mistakes over and over again. When we take ownership, we can then resolve to make better life choices the next time and move on. By doing this we learn, evolve and grow.

Above all, the most important thing I learned in the midst of my Life Changes was to forgive...Forgive my ex, but most of all, forgive myself. Hoarding hate and malice in your heart will stifle your happiness. Yes, I said it. FORGIVENESS . . . It's the greatest gift you can give yourself.

Chapter 23
What's Holding You Back?

Have you ever imagined what you could accomplish if you had no barriers? If there were no mountains standing in your way, what would you do? Would you live your life to the fullest, dream, create, and imagine, or would you sit idle watching life pass you by? I have always felt that life is the most beautiful, fantastic gift from God and it is just waiting to be opened and explored. But some of us are so afraid of the unknown that we allow the least little thing to hinder us. We already know from scripture that God did not give us the spirit of fear, so my question is: What is it that keeps YOU from realizing your greatness and prevents you from walking into your destiny?

Are you so afraid that you just might succeed? Or are you worried about what a few naysayers might say? Are you walking in your parents' footsteps and think just because mama didn't or daddy didn't, you won't either? Says who? Why not? Does it make you uncomfortable to try new and different things? Are you nervous when you step outside of your usual comfort zone? If so, that is a start. Welcome to Growth 101 where we live and let live!

Poet Marianne Williamson is quoted as saying, "Our deepest fear is that we are powerful beyond measure. It is our light, not our darkness, that most frightens us." I have always been one who chose to maximize my opportunities regardless of what anyone had to say or thought about me. Although there were times when I did try to hold back, I had to stop and ask myself why. Why did I feel the need to hold back in order to make someone else feel comfortable about *my* life? We only have one life to live, and if you have big dreams and aspirations, live them out! Sometimes we are our greatest enemies and it's time to stop working against yourself and start working for yourself.

While I agree that many of us need to get out of our own way, I have to say that for a lot of us, our biggest barriers are the people who we surround ourselves with; family and friends. Sometimes it's the opinions of complete strangers that we allow to stifle our growth. Oftentimes we allow the limitations and insecurities of others to become our roadblocks. This causes us to miss opportunities for growth. We cannot dim our lights to please others. What benefit does that serve us? Periodically, we need to sit down, be still and evaluate the people who surround us. And quite frankly, sometimes it's best if we give some of them an exit strategy from our lives.

For me, being positively upbeat and living my life to the fullest has caused many, many negative people to run as fast as they could in the opposite direction. Years ago I watched someone walk so fast out of my life that they literally hit the wall trying to get away from me. My energetic personality will send a negative person sprinting—even if they aren't a runner! LOL!!!

I dare you to try it. Overabundant optimism chases away >>>>>>>>>> pessimistic people.

Truthfully, everyone who comes into our lives isn't meant to stay in our lives, and we should be okay with that. We shouldn't be afraid to step out and be our own support if necessary. When I wanted to travel to Puerto Rico, I was told that was a crazy thought coming from a small town girl. I fail to see how my upbringing has anything to do with my aspirations. Therefore, not only did I vacation in Puerto Rico, I gave up my seat on my flight on the first trip and was given a roundtrip ticket to visit again within a year. And as of today, I have been three times! What God has for me belongs to this small town girl, and I refuse to let others hold me back or block my blessings.

This goes for you, too. What God has for you is for you, but you can't be afraid to go out and get it. And you definitely can't be afraid of telling "Negative Naysayers" and "Pesky Pessimists" to kick rocks. But even if you don't, your light will eventually blind them to the point they will be trying to exit stage left the same way the person who tried to discourage me did. Needless to say, the exit strategy was utilized and it worked. And guess what? Life goes on.

My dreams have always stretched far and wide, and so has the negativity of some of those surrounding me. I remember being told that going to Anchorage, Alaska to run in the Mayor's Midnight Sun Marathon was the craziest thing ever, not to mention going to Dublin, Ireland. But let me tell you; I had the best time ever on both of those trips, and I am so happy that I wasn't afraid or thought too small to do those things.

Sometimes people will discourage you from doing something for fear that you just might do it! Just because they want to stay stuck in the same spot does not mean you have to do the same. If the people around you won't change, change the people around you. Surround yourself with likeminded individuals, and connect with those who have similar dreams and aspirations. I've been connecting with movers and shakers since

Myspace days, and with the growth of social media, I don't see myself running out of means to bond with more likeminded individuals.

Through social media I have met a lot of really cool folks that have become good friends. I've connected with professionals who I met through clients I worked with in Marketing and Public Relations who have very similar dreams, drive and motivation as I do. I use every opportunity to network; book signings, business conventions, business socials, sporting events, and Chamber of Commerce events all over the world. Whenever I visit a city, I make it a point to attend chamber of commerce functions that are available to non-members, as well as visits to colleges or professional sporting events. I use these opportunities to exchange as many business cards as possible and shake as many hands as available. You never know what type of connection you can make, but you have to first seek out opportunities.

Through my networking I've enjoyed a relaxing Thursday morning meet up with friends in Greenwich Village for breakfast while visiting New York. I've had the pleasure of enjoying a winery tour in Napa Valley, California. It was a place I dreamed of visiting but had no idea how much fun it would be. I've had the pleasure of visiting quite a few times. I've taken Tae Bo Classes from Billy Blanks at his studio in Sherman Oaks, California, and taken a heavenly ride on the Staten Island Ferry and watched the awesome sight of Lady Liberty in the distance. I make it a habit not to limit myself. Just because events aren't typical for a "small town country girl," doesn't mean a small town country girl can't enjoy them. I've always wanted to see the world and its entire splendor. I don't let anything or anyone stop me from enjoying life's beauty.

Your life is yours to live and I encourage you to fill it with activities that stimulate growth and make you happy. Don't let the opinions of others influence the goals and dreams you have for yourself. Family and friends should bring value to your life, not try to bring you down because your glass is always half full and theirs is half empty. Honestly, happiness looks different for everyone, and that's why we should live and let live. We all have a different blueprint; your happy may not be my happy. No two are the same, so I urge you; BLAZE YOUR TRAIL! STEP OUT THE BOX! Don't fear your future, SEEK IT!

Chapter 24
Explore the Paths Less Traveled

"Monique, I like you more today than yesterday. Now go out and conquer your day with a smile," I said with enthusiasm as I smiled broadly at the beautiful reflection staring back at me.

As I reached for my floss, I could hear the wonderful words of wisdom coming from loved ones (who I affectionately deemed "my fan club") that I recited on a daily basis.

"Just be nice. Let God fight your battles," Mom often told me.

Granddaddy Frank told me, "Believe in yourself EVERY DAY!"

"Stay focused," was Grandma Tiny's often repeated phrase.

And Daddy's advice was, "Believe in your dreams and follow them through!"

This wonderful, loving group, along with a handful of other family members and friends, have always provided a positive motivational support system for me. Committed to living out my dreams, I grasp hold of every bit of their enthusiasm and I run with it!

When I turned 18, I was given a Bible and a set of luggage by my parents. "Because as sure as the sun rises in the east and sets in the west, you will be leaving Daddy's house to create your own life," my father told me. "We've given you the tools it takes to make it in life, now go out and show us your appreciation by becoming your very best."

My parents raised me and my siblings to believe that life had a lot to offer, and if we were willing to show dedication, work hard and stay prayerful, there were no limits to what we could achieve despite what anyone else had to say. I thank God for having parents who encouraged me and instilled positivity and strength into me, because there were a few people—family included— who did not want to see me succeed.

It always amazed me how people could pretend that they liked me in front of my parents, but showed contempt to my face when Mom and Dad were not present. As with all things in my life, I took a lesson from even those hurtful moments. I learned as a teen that some people are blessed to be born into great families, but others have to create them. We certainly can't pick and choose who God connects genetically, but some of the best families consist of friends that you *do* get to choose, and I'm blessed to have some dedicated, warm and loving friends who make up my extended family. They do as families should; accept, motivate and uplift. As for those naysayers . . . I made a promise to myself when I was 18 that I would use their disdain and negative energy to motivate and elevate me. So to them I say, "Thank you for being my footstool!"

I have a remarkable ability to tune out people's negative energy and not allow it to consume my thoughts or stifle my growth. I've never been one to let others get inside my head and make me second-guess my decisions or choices. Again, I wholeheartedly believe this has everything to do with the foundation my parents and grandparents laid. Grandma Tiny was fond of saying, "Life goes on with or without you. Stay in the race." And so I chose to stay the course. I'm not trying to outdo anyone; just trying to live the best life I know how.

Most people sit around year after year dreaming about what they could be doing and never doing it. Since my teenage years, I dreamed about doing so many things; traveling to new places and experiencing all kinds of adventures. Then I set out and lived my dreams. I dream and I do. That's just me, and it saddens me when I'm around empty people who have a problem with all of the things I have done in MY life. These same opportunities are available to all of us, so my advice is to get out there and experience life! And just in case you decide not to, please don't take your frustrations out on those of us who are. Because truthfully, we are too busy living life to the fullest to entertain your negativity anyway.

I'm happy! I'm inspired! I'm motivated! This is my life, my reality. I've created my own way through prayer and leaning on God's word. I can only suggest that others do the same. When you begin to motivate yourself daily, you will need very little motivation from others. Self-motivation builds you up and makes you strong, and quite often, your drive and motivation inspires others. Allow your motivation to stem from within and radiate on the outside. You never know who may be in need of a little sunshine in their lives.

Each new day brings about new opportunities to live out your life's dreams, but who says you have to wait until tomorrow? Life is amazingly beautiful, and as you create your own path, don't be afraid to explore the paths less traveled. You may be surprised at what you find awaiting you out there, and what new activities might catch your fancy. And even if the people surrounding you discourage you, find ways to motivate and encourage yourself! Find your own uplifting words and make them your mantra. But whatever you choose to do with your life; whether it's good or bad, remember the decision was yours. Live your life and allow others around you to live out theirs as well.

Chapter 25
Race to the Finish Line

When I was a child my parents always made sure that my birthdays were special and included some type of celebration. My father would stress the importance of celebrating birthdays, and I thank him for instilling this in me, because I was able to put his words into practice at one of the most crucial points in my life.

Daddy always told us, "Your birthday is the only day of the year that you own. Own it and enjoy it. You have the right to get all the attention, gifts and love you desire." And so I did. I never let a birthday go by without a celebration. For each of my birthdays I tried to think of unique and fun ways to commemorate and own my special day.

On January 15th, I was on a flight from Atlanta, Georgia to Phoenix, Arizona to take part in the P.F. Chang Rock N' Roll half marathon. It was in celebration of my upcoming birthday. In four short days I would turn 40 years old! As the old saying goes, "Life begins at 40." While I was looking forward to reaching this milestone, there was a certain sorrow that surrounded the 40th year; as it was the day after her 40th birthday that my older sister Lisa lost her battle with liver disease.

On the flight to Phoenix I decided that as a special tribute to Lisa, I would celebrate my birthday all year long. She did not have the opportunity to own her birthday that year, so in memory of her, I would own and enjoy the entire year for both of us.

As was a practice, the first thing on my agenda when the New Year came in was to mail out birthday reminder flyers to my family and close friends. Yes, I absolutely did. On the second day of January I put my reminders in the mail so that everyone would have enough time to mail off my gifts of money, cards and presents so they would arrive by my birth date. I also let them know that birthday phone calls were acceptable from little children and senior citizens. However, I fully expected to receive *something* on my birthday.

After I had mailed out my reminders, I geared up for the half marathon. True enough I planned the marathon as a way to commemorate my birthday, but the training also provided me with a great way to stay in shape; as it was 13.1 miles of terrain through beautiful Phoenix, Tempe and Scottsdale, Arizona. There was extensive training involved, but I loved it and was excited to have the opportunity to participate.

I remember sitting on the plane thinking about how this run would be my first birthday celebration. I was embarking on this trip alone and I was determined to treat myself without any regrets. This would be the first of many 40th year celebrations, and I couldn't wait to get started planning for the next one. But first I had to tackle the run.

I arrived in Phoenix three days before the race so I could get my body acclimated to the climate. When I arrived at the hotel, I met a small group of ladies who were from Spokane, Washington. Through our conversation I found out it was customary for them to run a few marathons a year. They used these events as a sort of *girl time retreat* where they could come together and fellowship with one another. A few of them had plans to run the full marathon, and some of them were going to run the half. They were a fun loving group of ladies, and at the end of our conversation they asked if I would like to join them for dinner. I gladly accepted. After dinner I took their information so that we could stay in touch, but unfortunately my luggage was lost on the flight home. Along with my luggage, I lost their contact information. But I never forgot those wonderful, friendly ladies who were unknowingly a part of my first 40th birthday celebration.

The Rock N' Roll Marathon was a great kickoff celebration, but once I left Phoenix, it was on to my next celebration; my *Forever 21 Tea Party!* My tea party was being held at the end of January in Florida. It was hosted at a beautiful, quaint tea room that was owned by one of my classmates. I sent out invitations to all the women who had made a positive impact in my life over the years. Of course, my guest of honor was my fun-loving mother. She was and continues to be such a ray of sunshine with her constant laughter and zest for life, which I inherited. Dad, on the other hand, is more laid back and thinks all of my ZEST makes me a fruitcake with lots of nuts☺. But it was his insistence on celebrating birthdays that sent me off on my yearlong celebration. So kudos to Dad, but the tea party was a ladies only event.

For my tea party, I asked each woman present to bring me $5.00 to cover the cost of a tip, and everything else on the tab would be picked up by yours truly, the birthday diva!

In the midst of celebrating my birthday, I wanted to celebrate each and every one of the ladies who made up my support system. During the event, I did a short speech thanking them individually for being an inspirational part of my life and journey, and then I presented each of the ladies with a copy of my motivational journal. We had such a great time talking, laughing and catching up. I made sure that everyone left the event knowing they'd made a positive impact on my life and that I was grateful for their presence.

For every subsequent month through December, I enjoyed a birthday gala of some sort. My friends and family were gracious enough to pitch in and help me carryout my yearlong celebration. Some of them were even nice enough to host the celebration. I'm sure some thought it was over the top, but I believe a lot of them had as much fun as I did planning and attending these 40th year celebrations.

Among the celebrations I shared with friends and family were a Fabulous February Flight celebration hosted at the 57th Fighter Group Restaurant in Atlanta. This was an enjoyable event complete with a brunch and helicopter run over the city with my family. I celebrated March in Monrovia, California with a fabulous workout luncheon held at a gym. April's awesome celebration was spent at the Final Four, of course, and my Marvelous May celebration was a dinner with friends in Pasadena, California. In June and July I hosted beach parties on Cocoa Beach in

Florida, and Venice Beach in California. Friends and family enjoyed a splashing good time barbecuing on the beach.

One of my favorite events was my bookstore birthday celebration. I met a group of friends at a Starbucks inside of a bookstore. They gave me an hour to find 40 soft cover, easy read, motivational books that they would pay for. It was like a super scavenger hunt! I had so much fun running around the store hunting down books and laughing with my friends. And yes, I successfully completed my task.

After that it was off to the windy city of Chicago to enjoy a pizza party with friends. After the party we attended a wonderful play in the city. October consisted of a Bowling Birthday celebration that was hosted by one of my favorite cousins, and November's party was spent at NASCAR Richard Petty Driving Experience. Now that was pure unadulterated fun and gave me a serious rush!

Closing out the year was a nice Christmas celebration spent at home with my family. I couldn't think of a better way to close out the most exhilarating year of my life than surrounded by my closest loved ones. Not only did I celebrate Lisa's and my 40th year, I learned a valuable life lesson over the course of that year; that we should treat every day like it's our birthday. We should enjoy and own each new day we are blessed to see.

I believe every day is a new opportunity to celebrate life and do something different. Even when we make mistakes, that does not mean life is over. It just means we have to make adjustments. I have difficulties just like everyone else, but instead of always getting down on myself or ducking my head in the sand, I choose to see the lesson for what it is and make the decision to do better the next time.

None of us are perfect. It's inevitable that we will stumble and fall at some point, but we must get back up. We must keep pushing forward and keep celebrating life. Every day is a gift. Don't just sit and watch your gift; tear that darn wrapper off of it and enjoy it! And while you're enjoying your life, you will look up one day and realize you are steadily moving forward . . . One step at a time . . . Racing Toward the Finish Line!

Chapter 26
One Helping Another

There is a scripture in the Bible that I take with me everywhere I go and I allow it to guide the most important part of me; my heart. Luke 12:48 reads: *"To whom much is given, much will be required,"* and I take my responsibility as a servant very seriously. I was raised to appreciate and utilize every blessing I've been given, and it is my duty to use them to be a blessing to others. Not only do I consider it my job, I actually love being able to reach out and help those in need. I've learned over the years that when you help others, it elevates you as well.

Helping others doesn't always have a price attached to it; things like a shoulder to lean on, a listening ear, smiling, and other small acts of kindness will take you farther than you can ever imagine. It doesn't cost one red cent to come out of your own small, little world and come to the aid of someone in need.

As a young girl growing up, I had the best examples to follow. I looked up to my big sister, Lisa, and her best friend, Veronica Johnson-Seget. Veronica has always been like a big sister to me and she looked out for me and allowed me to hang out with her. She was such a kind person. It was her and another friend, Marla Boone-McCray (who I lovingly referred to as my beauty queen older sister), who taught me real kindness and how to speak in love to others. These ladies have given me many years of friendship and laughter; from allowing me to tag along to Super Bowl events all over the country, to Marla sharing her helpful solutions to every beauty flaw under the sun. They have been a wealth of knowledge and I have no qualms about proudly walking in their shadows. Marla's beauty secrets and Veronica's kind hearted, helpful ways will impact me for the rest of my life, as I will always work to pay their kindness forward.

Sometimes all a person needs is for someone to offer them a listening ear. As small as this may seem, it is really hard to find someone who will just sit and listen with a loving spirit; passing no judgment or talking over you. I believe sometimes we get so absorbed with our own lives that we don't pay attention to things that are going on around us. There are so many opportunities to make an impact on someone's life if we would only learn to slow down and take in our surroundings. There are a great number of people out there who may need a helping hand and may not be able to verbalize it for one reason or another. I've been able to help two young ladies on two separate occasions who were victims of sex trafficking by not only being aware of my surroundings, but more importantly, being willing to get involved and help someone in need.

In 2009 while driving on I-85 headed to Charlotte, North Carolina, I was approaching my exit when I noticed a young girl around the age of 12 in the car next to me. She appeared to be trying to make eye contact with me. The adult male who was driving the car attempted to pull her closer to him and I could tell that something was not right. I did not allow him to catch me looking, but instead just dialed 911 from my Bluetooth and explained to the operator what had taken place. I slowed down just enough to get the license plate of the vehicle and stayed on the phone and in view of the vehicle until the nearest police officer could reach them. The driver exited the interstate and pulled into a QuikTrip. The police officer showed up and questioned both the man and the young girl. Sure enough, that child had been abducted from Washington D.C. By being aware of my surroundings, I was able to extend a helping hand to a child in need. For me that is what life is all about.

On another occasion in 2010, as I was traveling in Dallas, Texas, I was behind a vehicle stopped at a traffic light. As I sat there waiting for the light to change, I noticed the driver of the car, an adult male, watching me through his rearview mirror. I thought it was strange that he was watching me, and then I noticed a piece of paper slowly easing its way out of the trunk of his car. I immediately figured someone must've been in the trunk the way the paper was coming out little by little. We happened to be traveling in the same direction and were stopped again at the next light, so I pulled up close enough to make out the words, HELP ME, on the paper. I dialed 911 and shared this information along with the license plate number. The little girl was a missing nine year old whose world was about to be turned into the worst nightmare ever. I was told a month after that incident by a former colleague in Houston, Texas that the same type of occurrence had taken place in the Midwest with a little boy around the same age.

Paying attention to your surroundings is very important because someone's life could be at stake. In both of these cases I felt like something was terribly wrong. And instead of turning my head the other way and "minding my own business," I followed my instinct and was able to help two little girls who desperately needed a helping hand.

Since my teen years, I have always wanted to help others in need, but I learned that periodically the helper will also need help. I remember in April 2010 I was preparing to leave Allen, Texas and move back to Atlanta after my job assignment ended. During the packing phase I became a bit overwhelmed because I was trying to get everything done in order to be able to attend the NCAA Final Four. I wasn't being very successful pulling everything together because there was a lot of work still to be done. Two of my very good friends, Corliss and Donna, had called to check on my progress. While I never said a word about being overwhelmed, they both could hear the exhaustion and sadness in my voice. Corliss offered to drive from Chattanooga, Tennessee to my home in Allen, Texas to help me finish getting my things packed and my car placed in storage. She and Donna came and we were able to accomplish everything needed. The next morning Donna and I enjoyed a relaxing ride to San Antonio while Corliss drove us safely to the Final Four. After a weeklong vacation, I flew back to Dallas and met my friend, Landon, who had flown in from Atlanta to help me drive my car back to Georgia. They never hesitated to reach out to lend a hand to a friend in need, and I thank God for blessing me with friends who I call family.

There are times when extending a helping hand saves lives, changes lives or simply changes the way a person views life. Then there are those times when that helping hand rescues some of us from our own fashion faux pas! I remember a situation that occurred a few years prior to the San Antonio Final Four when my friends extended much needed kindness to me that resulted in a priceless memory. One day I decided that I would start wearing sneakers, and of course my shoe of choice was going to be Nike. I thought it would be cool to wear a pair of Nikes because I had never owned a pair. I only wore high heel shoes and owned one pair of running shoes, so this was quite a step for me. I took a trip to the mall to purchase my Nikes and decided to go all in and purchase a matching outfit as well.

I was so proud of myself that I couldn't wait to show off my new fashion sense to my friends, because I would finally fit in at sporting events. We were attending an open basketball practice during the Final Four event. I went into the gym and sat down in the bleachers next to Corliss and Donna. I turned to Corliss and told her to check out my new Nikes. Both of my friends were excited to see me out of my high heels and dressed more relaxed and event appropriate.

Corliss asked about my Nikes with a confused look on her face. Donna was looking toward my backpack as if she expected them to materialize from inside my bag. I was baffled as to why they were confused.

My Nikes were on my feet! Corliss looked down at my feet for a while, and being the loving friend that she was, she kindly broke the news to me.

"Sweetheart, those aren't Nikes. They're New Balance."

My mouth fell open as I looked down at my new shoes. I surely thought they were Nikes because they had the "N" on the side. Didn't "N" stand for Nike? We laughed until we cried. Getting to share this moment with my friends—making loving, priceless memories— is what it's all about. Teaching me that Nikes are the shoes with the "swoosh" checkmark on the side, so I won't go out in public making a fool out of myself thinking I have on Nikes instead of New Balance, is what I call a loving act of kindness! LOL!

Another moment that I will always remember occurred in May 2009. I was headed to Lenox Square Mall in the Buckhead area of Atlanta when I noticed a young lady walking in the parking lot. As I was walking while talking to one of my police officer friends on the phone, I made eye contact with her as she passed by. Something in her eyes made me uncomfortable. As I turned to look at her after passing her up, something in my spirit didn't sit well. I continued to think about her as I shopped for my makeup. By the time I was finished it was getting dark and I asked a security officer to accompany me to my car. As I was driving off I saw the young lady again, but this time she was sitting on the side of Macy's on the pavement near a truck. I left the mall, but early the next morning before dawn, I drove to the mall again looking for her.

I didn't see her at first, but I continued to drive around the parking lot, and sure enough I found her. She was lying near the trash bins on the side of the mall. When she heard my vehicle, she eased further behind the dumpster and I noticed mice running near the area where she was. I stopped and rolled down my window and asked her to meet me in the food court at 10:00 a.m. We met and I found out that she was homeless and hungry, but I noticed her clothes were fairly clean. I found out through our conversation that she was simply down on her luck. She was a very nice, educated, young lady who had been laid off from her job back in December due to cutbacks. She had managed as long as she could, but both of her parents were deceased and she was their only child. She had never met any family members on either side of her family, so when times got hard, there was no one for her to turn to. She had survived by going to different gyms and getting weeklong memberships so she could take showers. She had been washing her clothing at the gym and hanging them over the dumpster to dry, praying all day that the trash truck would not come while she was away. She had worked out a system and knew what time to rise so she wouldn't get caught by security. She would go into the food court and eat samples right before lunchtime to try to fill her stomach. Oftentimes she would watch to see if people would leave food on tables, and she would get a bite here and there. She had managed to go undetected until I had taken notice of her.

Her name was Ari, and with a little help, she managed to find a part-time job. She still had a system, but it no longer consisted of sleeping behind the dumpsters at the mall. After finding a job, I helped her get into a shelter until she was able to afford a place. She would go to the local beauty school to get her hair done for little to nothing, so at least she wouldn't look homeless. I gave her clothing, shoes and personal items, a gift card for food and a month long Marta transportation pass to get started, and she was on her way to recovery!

Ari has been forever grateful, and today she has reclaimed her life and is doing just fine. I am so happy that I was placed in her path, because she really didn't need a handout, just a hand up!

This is why I always take a moment to assess my surroundings. I try not to rush through life, and I always try to keep my servant's heart active. Sometimes it doesn't cost a dime to make a difference in someone's life. If you aren't blessed financially, then you can always do those activities that don't have a cost attached to them. There are shelters and plenty of boys and girls clubs that could use a willing volunteer. It doesn't really matter how small you think your contribution is. Being in service to others and helping people nourishes your spiritual being, and I'm sure we all could use more good vibrations. Frankly, I don't know what I would be doing if I wasn't trying to help someone, because kindness, service and motivation is as much a part of my make-up as breathing. Even if you start small with a smile, hug, or a kind word, it will make a difference. Whatever you do, do so with a loving heart and expecting nothing in return but the satisfaction of knowing that you are making a difference in someone's life. God will bless you, and your heart will thank you.

Chapter 27
Myomectomy, Hysterectomy and Understanding

I recall learning a nursery rhyme when I was a little girl that says, "Sugar and spice and everything nice . . . That's what little girls are made of." But growing up in the country, I wasn't always sugar and spice and everything nice. While I definitely loved dressing up and having my hair and nails done, I had no problem whatsoever being a tomboy either; running around with my cousins, feeding hogs and other farm animals, and climbing trees while wearing a dress with dress shoes. But all in all, I absolutely love being a woman. It is a beautiful thing. I love being a sensitive, nurturing and undeniably feminine woman. But let's be clear; it's definitely not all sugar and spice and everything nice.

The fairytales never told us that as little girls age and mature, there would be certain bodily functions and transformations our bodies would go through that would cause pain, suffering and mental anguish for a lot of women. I was one of those women.

Being a woman is sometimes very difficult and tough, even without experiencing "medical" issues. We have this *wonderful* time of the month where our body goes through all sorts of undesirable changes while preparing itself for reproduction. So imagine when we go through our menses and have to deal with hormonal symptoms that sometimes start to manifest days before the arrival of our monthly, unwelcoming special guest. Stress and anxiety, acne, constipation, headaches, weight gain, diarrhea, mood swings—and the most dreaded—abdominal cramps, are just a handful of symptoms that occur in a woman's body approximately every 28 days. Now throw in painful fibroids (abnormal growths that develop on the uterus) and you have circumstances that make it almost impossible to maintain a normal, healthy career.

Working in Corporate America is tough in its own right, but when you are dealing with medical issues, it becomes that much harder. Many times no one is really concerned how you are feeling physically or emotionally, just as long as you show up to work and are productive at the job you are assigned. I remember many days going to work in agonizing pain, but I had to put on my 'A' game face. I had to mix and mingle at after hour socials, deliver training seminars, and oversee marketing for products and services; all while nursing back and abdominal pain. On those days I would take short breaks and go into the restroom to freshen up, praying for a quiet moment just to gather myself to go back out and complete the cycle over again. Pain or no pain, work had to be done. But through God's grace and mercy, I was able to survive this situation with my mind, body and career intact, because I was blessed with a supervisor who cared and showed compassion. His name was Steve Jones.

Steve had an entirely female office staff and an outside staff that consisted of both men and women. He cared a great deal about his staff members. He went out of his way to make sure we had the things we needed and were surrounded by a positive work environment. He called monthly staff meetings to stay in touch with his staff members and to find out what we had going on in our lives and how he could offer assistance. He made certain to find out the personal little details about each of us— such as our favorite foods and colors— so that we were treated as individuals. He would always have our preferred snacks available, and made sure our birthdays were celebrated with cake *and* a paid holiday, which I always took full advantage of.

Of course with our entire office staff being female, there were days when one or more of us would begin to act with unease and become sensitive. Steve was very in tune to these moments. He knew there would be a *close friend*—or should I say an *unwelcomed special guest?* — stopping by to visit for a few days. So he took extra special care with us during those times. There were occasions tensions would run pretty high in the office, so much so that even the outside maintenance team could feel the attitude shift. They stayed as far away as possible; giving us plenty of space, which was pretty hard to do considering our bodies began to get in sync with each other and our cycles would come only days apart.

Some days at the office were too funny because the guys would literally run from us. We were one big, diverse family who actually spent more time together than we did with our own families. Despite the monthly tension, we all got along well, and as unusual as it may sound, we never wanted our boss, Steve, to take days off or leave us. And he rarely did. Periodically he would take an extended lunch to balance out his long work hours, but for the most part, he hardly ever missed a day and managed to be right there with us; guiding and taking the best care of his team.

The ladies in the office called ourselves Steve's work wives, and whenever his extended lunches became too long, one of us would text him requesting to know his whereabouts. We took turns visiting his office just to chat about personal things, because he was very understanding. We knew that he had our best interest at heart. It was not unusual for him to leave the office and come back with chocolates for all of us. He never did for one without doing for the others.

Every month we had to turn in our requests for days off to Steve for the entire month. In September he would ask if we could turn our calendars in for the holidays because surely it took quite a bit of time to coordinate all the days off we requested. Steve somehow always managed to grant our requests. I don't remember there being a time when he wasn't able to "make it happen." He made sacrifices for us, and so in turn we also made sacrifices. It was because of his dedication to our team that I endured going through tremendous pain and suffering month after month. I will be the first to tell you that I don't do pain very well, but I managed to deal with it and all the pitfalls that come with lengthy, painful, menstrual cycles; frequently running to the restroom to double-check my clothing, having a purse full of feminine products at all times, and always thinking ahead to make sure there were no embarrassing accidents.

Any type of pressure on my abdomen caused me severe pain. I literally didn't want to eat because I knew I would eventually have to use the restroom. I was a mess! I started having headaches because I wasn't eating, and I simply grew weary of living that way from month to month. I didn't discuss my dilemma with anyone because I felt like it was my body and I had to make my own choices about what was best for me. I had to make a decision about my health, but I didn't want to let my team down by not being there to carry my weight.

I resolved to setting up a consultation with my doctor. He gave me a few options in terms of what type of surgery he could perform to solve my issues. At the end of the consultation, it was narrowed down to either a Hysterectomy or a Myomectomy. The Myomectomy had only a 50% chance of solving my problem.

Either way it went, I soon realized that surgery was inevitable. I didn't want to take off six weeks to recover, so I decided to take a chance with the Myomectomy, which had a recovery time of only two weeks.

The morning of my surgery was just like the others before it. I was in pain and still suffering from a steady menstrual flow. I had been given medication that had slowed it down and masked the pain a bit, so I was ready to get it over with. The surgery went well and there seemed to be no complications; no pain during recovery and I was finally able to relax and enjoy a holiday season. I had a wonderful New Year's, and Valentine's Day came and went with no issues. I was eating dinner and actually not having to think about the pain that would follow, and I was ecstatic!

I marched right into March and was preparing for the annual NCAA March Madness when an uninvited guest arrived on the scene and ruined my peace. She came in with no intentions of leaving; running faster than Usain Bolt and cramps jumping higher than an NBA player going up for a slam dunk.

I was in so much pain as I struggled to move about day after day. Getting home and going to sleep was all I cared about. The pain drained me physically, emotionally and took me way out of my character. Sadly, I was unable to attend the 2012 NCAA Final Four because of the pain I suffered; had tickets for both the men and the women's games. At work I once again tried to keep my 'A' game face on, but it was becoming increasingly harder. I would spend my lunch breaks in the backseat of my car lying down. I was truly having a tough time. For six months I went on like that; in severe pain and dealing with a steady flow of blood. I knew something had to be done, so I asked my doctor numerous questions until I was certain that a Hysterectomy was the only option. In reality it was unavoidable and finally it was scheduled for September 2013.

I did online research on the pros and cons of having a Hysterectomy. I called a few friends and family members, but I didn't have anyone close to me who had experienced what I was going through. I continued to reach out and do as much research as I could on my own. I set up an online Q & A to help me come to terms with what I would possibly have to face after surgery. I was able to gather a diverse group of women of all races and ages to create a conference call to assist me and educate several other women who I had met through my research period. I was determined to surround myself with a team of women who would be my fan club through this experience. I refused to do this alone, because I would have found a way to back out in the 11th hour, probably cancelling my appointment for surgery at the last minute.

I found out that many of the women had experienced trauma on top of trauma after their husbands had walked out on them due to their medical issues. Several of them talked about the lack of compassion and understanding they received, and it really made me wonder what would have happened if they had gotten sick with an illness or disease instead of just having female medical issues. Would the men have stayed and offered them the love and support they needed, or would they still be forced to seek a support system online? It saddened me to think of what these women had gone through, and I was glad I was part of their support system.

Thankfully I had an awesome circle of support that kept me positive. I would receive encouraging emails, text messages and phone calls from women all over the world. My coworkers were also very supportive, as they understood that my health was a priority and they were willing to pull the extra weight for the six weeks I would be out recovering. Steve, Nazila, Claudia, Claire and Melanie held things down for me in my absence, and I am forever thankful.

Needless to say, my second surgery was a success! I am so happy I made the decision to go through with it, because I no longer had the worries I carried with me for so long. I didn't miss anything about the monthly visits; not the inconvenience, the anxiety and definitely not the pain. My doctor recommended six weeks recovery time, but just to be on the safe side I extended my recovery period to six months. I wanted to make sure there would be no relapsing or complications, so I ceased all of my usual physical activities. I didn't go to the gym, lift weights, run or do anything overly physical for those six months. I know I made the right decision for me.

Through it all, I was able to remain positive and reassured. I focused all of my attention on getting better instead of worrying about work and other things that could wait. Through both of my surgeries there was a level of calmness that I can only surmise was due to the fact that I had a supervisor who was very supportive and understanding. His level of compassion as a male was astounding, and I can't begin to say how appreciative I am for being blessed with Steve. His spirit was amazing and he was every mother's dream!

The outpouring of love I received from my job kept me lifted, and even though I retired on August 1, 2014 and now have the freedom to sit and reflect on my years of service through marketing, retention management and training, my heart sings of the many wonderful people I worked with and for the opportunity to have Steve Jones as my supervisor.

I commend every woman who has had to endure the pain and stress of surgery, and I want to encourage the ones who are still dealing with medical issues. Take it from a person who cringes at the thought of pain; my ultimate medical decision for myself was well worth it. While it was not an easy process, I experienced a high level of comfort very soon after surgery. In fact, I was told that I was so comfortable, that I engaged in a hilarious conversation about college football after coming out of surgery. Being the sports fanatic I am, I wasn't surprised to hear that. But seriously, if you are battling the same type of issues I went through, I urge you to ask as many questions as you need to, do your personal research, and find a support system to keep you positive. I know it helped me a great deal.

I was blessed to receive not only encouraging words, but also flowers, visits, and many gifts as I recovered. And as always, my number one supporter was there holding my hand through the entire ordeal. Mom always comes through for me and helps me through the tough times, and I thank God she was there through both my Myomectomy and Hysterectomy. And I thank God for all the other angels who were the wind beneath my wings as well.

Chapter 28
Walk It Out

Over the last 10 years I have learned an overabundance of life lessons while journeying to that glorious place called Happy. In this chapter I will outline a few of my tried and true remedies for the little things that cause undue stress and strife in our lives. I've met too many young people over the years who are struggling with high blood pressure and other assorted ailments that are really tied to their mental health. I've come to realize if we just take a few extra precautions, many of these small medical and mental issues can be avoided. Some of these little gems have been passed on to me from Grandmother Tiny and my aunt Sue. They work for me, so of course I am going to share.

Some of us spend way too much time on the rough side of the mountain. Sometimes we get too comfortable wallowing in our self-pity and stuck in situations instead of finding a way to go through whatever we need to go through in order to get to the other side. Going through sometimes involves building a bridge and getting over whatever is causing undue stress. Some of us would rather sit around wasting precious time talking about our struggles instead of doing something about them. Why is that?

You should not be waiting for someone to change your life unless that someone is you! If you aren't happy, then make changes. Start thinking beyond where you are currently standing. Get up and move; walk it out one step at a time. And remember, change takes time, so as long as you are moving forward, thinking forward and looking forward, you're going in the right direction.

In the midst of your forward march, you must have compassion for yourself. Love yourself even when you don't feel like you are at your best. We all have struggles and will always have to face challenges, but never get complacent in your struggles. Always strive to be a better you than you were the day before. Sometimes this involves making small changes to your daily lifestyle. The next few tips may seem minute, but they can be beneficial in minimizing your overall stress level. If you are a person who is always running late, causing road rage because you are zooming in and out of traffic, then you need to:

- Get up 20 minutes earlier so you can leave home earlier.

- Gas up on your way home from work or the night before so you won't have to stop in the morning.

- If you get distracted by the television, don't turn it on. Listen to music or read an eBook instead.

- Set all of your home and vehicle clocks 7-11 minutes faster to help you with your time management.

- Place your alarm clock out of reach so you will not be able to hit the snooze button over and over (This will get under your skin at first and you will probably not like me for suggesting it, but it works!).

- Lay your clothes out the night before.

- Take the time to program three ICE (In case of Emergency) numbers into your cell phone so the police can have someone to contact in the event that something happens to you.

- Place any items that need to go with you the next morning in plain sight.

These simple tips are tried and true and should help you to jumpstart your day with ease. There are too many people struggling with nagging, trivial health issues because they simply fail to do the littlest of things that will help them become more organized and put less pressure on their health.

Stress is real and it causes real damage to your mind, body and spirit. We must learn to take better care and responsibility for our overall wellness. Just because your parents, aunts and uncles have high blood pressure and stress about any and everything, does not mean this has to be your story. Walk it out and do better for yourself by starting with your diet.

- Drink more water (add lemon to it if you need flavor).

- Make better choices about the food you eat.

- Eat smaller meals during the day.

- Eat more fresh fruits and vegetables.

I remember when I was a teenager and I would encounter a person who just seemed to have woken up on the wrong side of the bed; just mean and hateful for no reason. I used to think to myself, *They must be constipated and could use a good cleaning out.* I always laugh when I think about that, but really, it's no laughing matter. My aunt Sue and I were having one of our weekly phone conversations and I remember telling her I would soon be headed out to my annual colonic appointment. She said, "You young people are always wasting your money running to the doctor for every problem under the sun. You could save your money if you made good use of the wisdom in your family. Why would you spend money on a colonic when all you need is two tablespoons full of Epsom salt and take it with a cup of warm water?"

And so I did. And guess what? Three hours later I felt as light as a feather! When I was talking to her about soaking in Epsom salt after running the Bermuda Marathon, she suggested that I read the side of the Epsom salt bag to find other great uses for it. Aunt Sue also told me to drink two tablespoons of organic apple cider vinegar in a cup of cold water first thing in the morning to maintain good blood pressure and keep my bowels regular. She also suggested that I Google the benefits of apple cider vinegar to find out how it could benefit me in other ways.

I love talking to the elders in my family. They are so full of wisdom and great advice. Grandmother Tiny always spoke life into me every time we were together. She reminded me to love myself, love others, forgive and move on. Her advice was to always purposely work to light up the world by first starting to enjoy my own light. You have to ask yourself from time to time, "What can I do to help me?" My answer is to take good care of yourself. You are blessed with only one body and one chance at life. Celebrate your victories (large and small) and don't be afraid of what others might say about it. No one knows your story better than you, so when you overcome some type of adversity, pat yourself on the back and celebrate. Growth is not always easy, so as you live and grow, have compassion for yourself.

Now I caution you, in the midst of your growth, you will encounter some folks in your circle who will not understand. They will think you are getting too big for your britches instead of seeing your change as something positive. Many will take it personal. That is why elevating your mindset will oftentimes involve making changes to your circles. There are a lot of people whose vision doesn't extend beyond the next day, much less the next year or years! Their goals involve waking up and making it through the day. If that's not all you see for yourself, and if the people around you won't change, then change the people around you. Don't stifle your growth because those around you are stagnant. Simply find folks who are doing more and have already done whatever it is you are looking to do. Ask for help; seek out mentors and push forward—always! Don't waste your time thinking about it; get up and do it! You will be happy that you did.

Respect your time and the time of others. Time is something that we are unable to go and retrieve. We can't get it back or ever replace it, and that is why you have to make good use of it.

- If you make appointments, keep them or cancel them in time to give the person a chance to fill your slot.

- Arrive at appointments 15 minutes ahead of time in case there is paperwork to fill out.

- If you are going to be late, call ahead and let the person know.

And finally, bloom where you are planted. I cannot stress this enough. If circumstances place you in a particular place where you are not happy to be, what good will it do to whine, cry and complain about it? If your job sends you to Po Dunk, USA and that is where you have to call home for the next year, I suggest you bring a little sunshine to Po Dunk and keep it moving. Get out and meet people. Who knows, they might be feeling the same way. Put your heads together and find a way to shine while you are there. Whatever you do, just make sure you are moving forward, because no one wants to follow a parked car!

Chapter 29
On the 50 Yard Line

When I look back over my life and I think things over, I have an overwhelming urge to break out in my own version of the Happy Dance! I am joyfully thankful and absolutely thrilled that I have made it this far in life. I do not take my life or anything about it for granted. I recognize that not everyone has made it this far, and certainly not everyone has been able to see the places I've seen and experience the beauty of this world as I have. From the beautiful, yet simple moments when I am able to play on the floor with my great nephew, AJ, to the awe inspiring moments I was able to take in at the natural splendor of Niagara Falls and the breathtaking Venetian sunset, I can truly say I have lived my life to the fullest.

My reality is my reality, and while some will always think my eyes are too big, I am going to continue to dream big even when I am unable to see the light at the end of the tunnel—because I already know that light is there and I just have to make it through the darkness to reach it. I've never been afraid to go through, but I also have never been one to sit around and write an obituary to any event in my life. That is because I intentionally choose to speak life into every situation. I understand that life brings about challenges, and I must go through tests in order to soar through and watch God's many blessings manifest in my life. Through creating annual vision boards and online journaling, I have been able to see the goal and visualize the victory.

Like everyone, I've experienced the bad as well as the good, but unlike some people, I choose to focus on the positive memories that have shaped my existence. Journaling has been a large part of my life, and through this pursuit I am able to look back on some really fantastic and uplifting moments on those days when I need an emotional lift. I have one journal in particular I titled "Happy," because it is full of beautiful, happy memories. It is that one journal that has the ability to pick me up when no one around me knows exactly what I am experiencing. It always takes me back to another place and shows me the light of things already done and helps me to create more memories. Some of the more memorable events in the journal are my weekend getaways to the Biltmore Estates, Smokey Mountains, and Martha's Vineyard where I went to spend quality time with myself; simply some "me time" to get into my own space.

In my Happy Journal, I've documented some great times over the past ten years that have the ability to transform even the gloomiest of days.

Sometimes when I am not feeling my usual bubbly self, I can scroll to a date and reflect on a memory that lets me know how truly blessed I am. Within the pages of my Happy Journal, I can find numerous funny family moments, like when I documented the time during elementary school when I changed my name. What a hilarious story!

When school started, I met so many little girls with the name Tonya who I thought were cute girls. My daddy had always told me I was cute, so in my mind, I just figured my mom accidentally gave me the wrong name. Cute girls were named Tonya, not Monique. Makes sense, right? So of course I started telling all the other students my name was Tonia; spelled with an 'I.' I only forgot to tell my parents.

Well, one day Mom went to the grocery store after work, only to come home with no groceries. Daddy asked her what happened and I stood in my bedroom listening as she told him.

"This little girl chased me around the store telling me to tell my daughter, Tonya, 'hello,' and that she would see her in school on Monday," my mother said. "I told her, 'Sweetie, I don't have a daughter named Tonya.' And she said, 'Yes, ma'am, you do. And she spells her name T-O-N-I-A, and mine is spelled T-O-N-Y-A. She wears her hair in two afro puffs.'" Mom went on to say, "I got so tired of that little girl following me up and down the aisles until I just left the cart and came home!"

I ran out of my room and said, "Mom, was it a little blonde headed girl named Tonya?" Mom answered yes and I proceeded to tell her and Daddy that I had officially changed my name to Tonia. My parents were both speechless, so I took that as a sign that it was okay. I can't remember how long my Tonia phase lasted, but I know the memory of that day always makes me smile, as does my childhood Easter memories.

When I was little I would learn a speech to recite in church on Easter Sunday. On the night before, I would stand in front of Mom and recite it for her so I would be ready. Grandmother Chandler always told me to smile throughout my speech and to look around the room at everyone as I spoke. If folks were nodding their heads, that meant I was doing good and they were supporting me. I loved standing up in front of the small group of church members in my pretty Easter dress. My favorite colors were pink, green, purple and white, and I always wore black shoes and carried a black purse. Even when I messed up, the adults would praise me, and the great part about Easter was that Daddy always made sure my Easter basket was waiting for me when I got home. These warm family memories have the ability to make me smile even during the most trying times.

I always try to find the chapters in my life that have brought me the most joy. By the time I am finished reminiscing on my classic Monique Moments, I am usually smiling, laughing or crying from sheer joy. Some of the most beautiful memories involve co-parenting my nephews after my sister, Lisa, passed away. I know I got on their nerves with my no-nonsense auntie/mother discipline, but I only wanted the best for them because they are my hearts of joy and I love them dearly. Thoughts of them and their mom always bring a smile to my face.

When I am missing my sister, I think back to the days when she would take me with her to her high school events. She was in the band, and one night after a band event, my brothers, Big D and Rusty, and I really wanted to stay and spend time with Lisa, but we had to go home. I still have the funniest picture of all four of us crying with our poker faces. It speaks volumes about our relationship, and I can always feel her warmth when I look at that picture.

Speaking of high school, I have a funny memory of the time I decided to try out for the cross-country team. Quite naturally I thought I was going to make the team because my last name was Chandler and Chandlers were known to be remarkable athletes. Daddy tried to warn me that I would not like cross country, but I wouldn't listen. He didn't want to hurt my feelings by telling me the truth, which was that I just was not athletic, but I did not catch the hint. I did really well on the first day, but day two was quite a bit different. We were supposed to run the trail through the woods behind the school, but that wasn't happening for me. I made it through lap one, but on the second lap, I ran into the woods and took a badly needed rest break.

I waited for the group to come past, and on their last lap, I rejoined them and made it across the finish line with a great time. Coach Loper just smiled and said, "Great job, team!"

Some years later Coach was hospitalized and I went to visit him in the hospital in Florida. He was asleep when I arrived, but when he woke up and saw me, he asked me a question that never fails to make me smile. He said, "Are you still hiding in the woods?" I was so shocked because I had no idea that in all these years he knew about my rest break.

I answered him back, "No. I'm a champ. I face challenges head on, and if I don't succeed the first time, I try again until I make it!"

Funny thing is, Dad and Coach Loper already knew I wasn't an athlete, but they let me figure that out on my own, just like I had to finally realize that I could not pull the wool over Mom's eyes no matter how hard I tried.

When I was in high school, I called home one night right before midnight curfew to tell my mom that I had a flat tire. The rule was to be home before the alarm clock went off; otherwise you were in for it! I called ten minutes before the alarm was set to go off because I wanted to hang out after the football game in a McDonald's parking lot with my cousins. When I called home and told Mom about the "flat tire" I had, she sweetly told me to be careful after I assured her one of the managers at McDonald's would change the tire for me.

I hung up the phone, exited the phone booth, and walked back to chat with my cousins. I was so sure I had gotten over. Fifteen minutes later as I was laughing with my cousins, my mom pulled into the parking lot on two wheels. I was shocked as I watched her screech to a halt and jump out the car with a jack in her hands. She told me it was time to pack up and head home as she proceeded to jack up the car. And as if that wasn't enough, a few minutes later Daddy rolled into the parking lot to finish up the job.

Mom told Daddy to put the tire in the trunk of her car as I said goodnight to my cousins and headed home with Mom. The next morning I woke up to the delicious smell of breakfast cooking. Mom walked into my bedroom and told me that breakfast was ready and to enjoy it. About 45 minutes later she came into the kitchen as I was finishing up and said good morning again, but this time with a cat-that-ate-the-canary look on her face. She looked me right in the eye and said, "By the way, you should be good to go. I had the tire looked at this morning and there was nothing wrong with it EXCEPT someone let the air out of the tire." She had that look on her face that let me know she was not fooled and that she already knew I had let the air out so I could stay out past curfew. I learned my lesson that day to never let the alarm clock catch me!

I love being able to reflect on happy memories with my family. My parents have always been supportive and loving. Sometimes I love for all of us to get together and treat ourselves. Occasionally we will dress up and go out to a nice, fancy restaurant just because. Recently, my parents and I met my absolute favorite cousin, Harrington, and his wife Patricia, at one of my favorite restaurants in Atlanta, Fogo de Chao. We celebrated just being able to look one another eye to eye and say, "I love you." A few of my favorite people having dinner at one of my favorite places is my definition of a night to remember.

I thank God for family, because they provide me with so many happy memories and laughter, like the time my niece wanted a bowling party for her second birthday. Imagine a two year old with bumpers and a ramp to bowl. Of course her dad or Papa had to place the ball on the ramp for her. She really thought she was doing it up. She was jumping up and down like she was bowling strikes when only one pin would fall. It was too funny!

Through the years I've also had the pleasure of meeting some awesome and amazingly beautiful people outside of family. I've met people from all walks of life who have contributed to my most happy memories. I remember one occasion when I decided to do something nice for myself and ended up a star for a night. I planned a date for myself on Valentine's Day that included renting a gown and purchasing a Diana Ross wig. I had my makeup done and I rented a limousine to pick me up and take me to the Abbey Restaurant, which was once St. Paul Presbyterian Church on Ponce de Leon Avenue in Atlanta. The restaurant sat on the corner of a major intersection and it was always busy, so there were lots of folks milling around. The limo driver pulled up to the restaurant and gave me the star treatment. He opened my door, and when I got out, there were people staring and making comments.

I heard a guy say, "That's Diana Ross, and she looks beautiful!"

I felt like a million bucks, so I played my part by blowing the crowd a kiss, then proceeded to sashay into the restaurant like I was the R&B diva herself. When I got to my table, there were a dozen red roses that I had ordered waiting for me. With the limo driver walking me to my table as if he was my bodyguard, the fantasy was complete. I was the center of attention. The entire wait staff came over to say hello, and all the other guests were dumbstruck trying to figure out who this famous person was. After dinner, the limo driver once again came in and escorted me out.

As I was leaving I heard someone say, "Excuse me, ma'am, would you mind if I take a picture with you?"

I told him, "It would be my pleasure."

I had taken a photo with two of the most gorgeous guys, and soon after, all I saw were flashes and voices saying, "It's her. It's Diana Ross!"

When I got in the limo, the driver looked at me and smiled. "They really thought you were Diana Ross," he said as he pulled away from the curb. When he dropped me off, he told me, "You made my night. There's no charge for driving you around."

Now that made *my* night, and goes down in history as one of the best nights ever that did not include family; just wonderful people.

There was another time I can remember when I was on assignment in Allen, Texas. There was this guy who walked up to me as if he knew me. I immediately got on the defense and my martial arts skills almost kicked in. He must've seen the look in my eyes, because he quickly explained that I looked like a lady he knew in Gwinnett County, which was located outside of Atlanta. I smiled and said, "Really?"

He went on to say, "Yes. She housed our professional hockey players."

I laughed because I knew he was talking about me. I had been the Marketing Director for a high end multi-family property management company. One of my duties had been setting up corporate housing for professional athletes, which included hockey players. I enjoyed attending ice hockey matches with my friends in Atlanta and would go as often as I could. I always loved how cool it was inside the arena when the Thrashers were playing.

After I confirmed that I was the person he thought, he asked what I was doing in Texas. I explained that I was working on an assignment requested by my corporate office. Out of nowhere he gave me free tickets to a professional hockey game. He gave me so many tickets that I was able to bring a group of Allen High School football players, members of One Community Church, and some nice folks I had met at a neighborhood Kroger grocery store. We had an awesome time and I relished the moments spent with people I had just met, sharing a good ole hockey game.

I guess you could say I am a "people friendly person," because I love meeting new people and sharing new experiences. I know there are some not so nice folks out there, because I have run across quite a few in my lifetime. But I also know none of us are perfect and never will be. We will always have some good days and we will have our share of bad days, but we all have it in us to make a choice to find our happy place.

If you can, travel and see the world or at least another state. I remember getting together with a group of friends; Alexis, Ashton, Meagan, Meredith, Caleb, Joeley, Morgan, Chuck, Garrison, Dekota and Patrick. We took a road trip. We took a vacation and visited Lewiston, Maine, Providence, Rhode Island and Burlington, Vermont. We stayed at each location for a few days; renting a house and just having some good, old fashioned fun! The trip was taken in mid-September when the weather was heavenly. We were able to walk around the cities during the day, and we rented a car service at night. It was so great just being able to relax and sightsee. There was plenty of laughter and precious memories made on this journey.

Happy times are so important to your wellbeing. It's so much easier to smile and be at ease than to worry and carry the weight of the world on your shoulders. Every day that we are able to open our eyes and breathe in God's blessed air means we are granted another day to be alive and live! If you are happy, then congratulations on being connected with your happy. If you're not, I urge you to start connecting today. There's nothing like it! I thank all of the amazing and awe inspiring folks who I've met on my journey, because I've had some of the best experiences that have made a lasting impression on me. I've been loved, supported and encouraged by some of the best. As a person who is definitely connected to her happy, I want to see the world happy.

My wish is that each of you continues to go hard in the paint to make positive changes in your lives. High jump over those pesky hurdles, and every now and then when you set-up, smack it out just to prove to yourself that you can do it. Make it to the 50 yard line and keep pushing into the end zone. But most of all, if you make it to third base, go ahead and make a run for it. Slide right into home and make that homerun. You can do it! I believe in you! You got this thing called life. Now do your best to become your very best and WIN!

www.ingramcontent.com/pod-product-compliance
Lightning Source LLC
Chambersburg PA
CBHW071213090426
42736CB00014B/2806